CONTINENTS IN CLOSE-UP

ASIA

MALCOLM PORTER and KEITH LYE

CHERRYTREE BOOKS

A Cherrytree Book

Designed and produced by
A S Publishing
Text by Keith Lye
Illustrated by Malcolm Porter and Raymond Turvey

First published 2001
by Cherrytree Press
327 High Street
Slough
Berkshire
SL1 1TX

© Malcolm Porter and A S Publishing

British Library Cataloguing in Publication Data

Porter, Malcolm
    Asia. - (Continents in close-up)
    1.Children's atlases
    2.Asia - Maps for children
    I.Title II.Lye, Keith
    912.5

ISBN 1 842 34028 X

Printed in Hong Kong

CONTINENTS IN CLOSE-UP

ASIA

This illustrated atlas combines maps, pictures, flags, globes,
information panels, diagrams and charts to give an overview
of the whole continent and a closer look at each of its countries.

COUNTRY CLOSE-UPS

Each double-page spread has these
features:

Introduction The author introduces the
most important facts about the country or
region.

Globe A globe on which you can see the
country's or region's position in the
continent and the world.

Flags Every country's flag is shown.

Information panels Every country has an
information panel which gives its area,
population and capital, and where possible
its main towns, languages, religions,
government and currency.

Pictures Important features of each
country are illustrated and captioned to
give a flavour of the country. You can
find out about physical features, famous
people, ordinary people, animals, plants,
places, products and much more.

Maps Every country is shown on a clear,
accurate map. To get the most out of the
maps it helps to know the symbols which
are shown in the key on the opposite
page.

Land You can see by the colouring on
the map where the land is forested,
frozen or desert.

Height Relief hill shading shows where
the mountain ranges are. Individual
mountains are marked by a triangle.

Direction All of the maps are drawn with
north at the top of the page.

Scale All of the maps are drawn to scale
so that you can find the distance between
places in miles or kilometres.

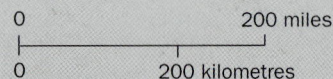

0	200 miles
0	200 kilometres

KEY TO MAPS

INDIA	Country name
Kashmir	Region
~~	Country border
■	More than 1 million people*
•	More than 500,000 people
·	Less than 500,000 people
□	Country capital
HINDU KUSH	Mountain range
▲ *Everest 8848m*	Mountain with its height
∴ *Petra*	Archaeological site

Mekong	River
⊢⊢⊢	Canal
🝔	Lake
⊢	Dam
🝔	Island

	Forest
	Crops
	Dry grassland
	Desert
	Tundra
	Polar

*Many large cities, such as Izmir, have metropolitan populations that are greater than the city figures. Such cities have larger dot sizes to emphasize their importance

CONTINENT CLOSE-UPS

People and Beliefs Map of population densities; chart of percentage of population by country; chart of areas of countries; map and chart of religions.

Climate and Vegetation Map of vegetation from forests to deserts; chart of land use; maps of summer and winter temperatures; map of annual rainfall.

Ecology and Environment Map of environmental damage to land and sea; panels on damaging the environment, natural hazards and endangered species; map of natural hazards.

Economy Map of agricultural and industrial products; pie-chart of gross national product for individual countries; panel on per capita gross national products; map of sources of energy.

Politics and History Map of great Asian empires; panel on great events; timeline of important dates; map of important events.

Index All the names on the maps and in the picture captions can be found in the index at the end of the book.

CONTENTS

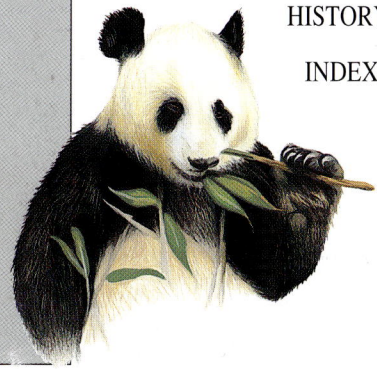

Giant panda
see page 20

ASIA

Asia is the largest of the continents, covering about three-tenths of the world's land area. It has more people than any other continent, with about three-fifths of the world's total population. Stretching from the icy Arctic in the north to the hot and steamy equatorial lands in the south, Asia contains huge empty deserts, as well as many of the world's highest mountains and longest rivers.

A long, mainly land border in the west separates Europe from Asia. This boundary runs north-south down the Ural Mountains in Russia, along the Ural River to the Caspian Sea and then through the Caucasus Mountains to the Black Sea. About three-quarters of Russia lies in Asia, while the rest is in Europe. Small parts of four other Asian countries also lie in Europe.

Cuneiform was an early form of writing. The wedge-shaped inscriptions were used around 5,000 years ago by the ancient Sumerian people, who founded a great civilization in the Tigris-Euphrates region in what is now Iraq. Several major civilizations developed in Asia.

Religions Asia was the home of all of the world's eight major religions. Hinduism is an ancient religion of India, as also is Buddhism, which was founded about 2,500 years ago. Judaism, Christianity and Islam developed in southwest Asia. Confucianism and Taoism were originally founded in China, while Shinto is a Japanese religion.

Rice is the chief food crop in the hot and rainy parts of Asia. The world's top eight rice producers are in Asia. In order of importance, they are China, India, Indonesia, Bangladesh, Vietnam, Thailand, Myanmar (Burma) and Japan.

R

KAZAKHSTAN

TURKEY
GEORGIA
ARMENIA
AZERBAIJAN
CYPRUS
UZBEKISTAN
KYRGYZSTAN
LEBANON
SYRIA
TURKMENISTAN
TAJIKISTAN
ISRAEL
JORDAN
IRAQ
IRAN
AFGHANISTAN
KUWAIT
SAUDI
ARABIA
BAHRAIN
QATAR
PAKISTAN
NEPAL
BHU
UNITED
ARAB
EMIRATES
BANGLAD
INDIA
OMAN
YEMEN
SRI LANKA
MALDIVES

ASIA

Area: 44,709,500sq km (17,262,400sq miles)
Population: 3,527,349,000
Number of independent countries: 48
(including Russia, Azerbaijan, Georgia, Kazakhstan and Turkey, which lie mostly in Asia)

Tigers live mainly in southern and southeastern Asia, but because of hunting and the destruction of the habitats where they once roamed free, they are an endangered species. Poachers kill tigers for their skins, bones and other body parts which are used to make potions in parts of Asia.

Great Wall of China This is the longest structure ever built. It is about 7,400 km (4,600 miles) long. Construction probably began in the 5th century BC and continued until the 17th century AD. The wall protected China from invaders from the north.

Poverty is widespread in Asia. Most countries depend on farming, but some have grown rich through manufacturing and trade. The Petronas Towers in Kuala Lumpur, Malaysia, are a symbol of Southeast Asia's increasing prosperity.

RUSSIA
MONGOLIA
NORTH KOREA
SOUTH KOREA
JAPAN
CHINA
TAIWAN
MYANMAR
LAOS
THAILAND
VIETNAM
CAMBODIA
PHILIPPINES
BRUNEI
MALAYSIA
SINGAPORE
INDONESIA

RUSSIA AND THE CAUCASUS

Russia is the world's largest country. About three-quarters of it lies in Asia, east of the Ural Mountains and the Caspian Sea. The rest is in Europe. From 1922 Russia was the centre of the Communist USSR (Union of Soviet Socialist Republics), known as the Soviet Union. In 1991 the Soviet Union split up into 15 countries.

Three of these countries – Armenia, Azerbaijan and Georgia – border Russia in the southwest. Together they are called Transcaucasia after the high Caucasus Mountains that lie to the north. Conflict has occurred in Chechnya, Russia, and also in parts of Transcaucasia, as rival ethnic and religious groups have fought for independence.

Woolly mammoths lived during the Ice Age in Siberia (a name often used for Asian Russia). They died out about 10,000 years ago, but bodies of mammoths have been found perfectly preserved in the frozen subsoil of Siberia.

RUSSIA

Area: 17,075,400sq km (6,592,850sq miles), of which about 75% is in Asia
Highest point: Mount Elbrus, in the Caucasus Mountains, 5,642m (18,510ft)
Population: 147,307,000 (about 20% of whom live in Asian Russia)
Capital and largest city: Moscow (pop 8,400,000)
Other large cities (in Asian Russia):
Novosibirsk (1,418,000)
Yekaterinburg (1,347,000)
Omsk (1,161,000)
Chelyabinsk (1,125,000)
Krasnoyarsk (914,000)
Irkutsk (632,000)
Official language: Russian
Religions: Christianity (Russian Orthodox 16%), Islam 10%
Government: Republic
Currency: Rouble

Oil and natural gas are abundant in Russia, and the country is a major producer. Azerbaijan also has large oil deposits in the Caspian Sea. Russia has most of the minerals it needs, including bauxite, copper, diamonds, iron ore, nickel and phosphates (used to make fertilizers).

GEORGIA

Area: 69,700sq km (26,911sq miles), 21% of which is in Europe
Highest point: Mt Shkhara 5,201m (17,163ft)
Population: 5,427,000
Capital: Tbilisi (pop 1,253,000)
Official language: Georgian
Religions: Christianity (46%), Islam (11%)
Government: Republic
Currency: Lari

ARMENIA

Area: 29,800sq km (11,506sq miles)
Highest point: Mt Aragats 4,090m (13,419ft)
Population: 3,787,000
Capital: Yerevan (pop 1,283,000)
Official language: Armenian
Religions: Christianity (Armenian Apostolic 65%, other Christian 13%)
Government: Republic
Currency: Dram

AZERBAIJAN

Area: 86,600sq km (33,436sq miles), 17% of which is in Europe
Highest point: Bazar Dyuzi 4,466m (14,652ft)
Population: 7,600,000
Capital: Baku (pop 2,500,000)
Official language: Azerbaijani
Religions: Islam (93%)
Government: Republic
Currency: Manat

Joseph Stalin (1879-1953) was born in Georgia. He played a leading part in the 1917 Russian Revolution, which turned Russia into a Communist country. From 1929 until his death in 1953, Stalin was the dictator of the Soviet Union. His rule was marked by great brutality.

0 ____ 500 miles

0 ____ 500 kilometres

Wrangel Island

East Siberian Sea

Severnaya Zemlya

New Siberian Islands

Bering Sea

Kara Sea

Laptev Sea

Dickson

Nordvik

Kolyma Mts

Kamchatka Peninsula

Indigirka

Verkhoyansk Range

Lena

Central Siberian Plateau

Magadan

Okhotsk

Petropavlosk-Kamchatskiy

Yenisey

R U S S I A

Yakutsk

Sea of Okhotsk

Stanoyoy Range

Sakhalin

Kiril Islands

lain

Komsomolsk

Tomsk

Kemerovo

Bratsk

Yablonovyy Range

Amur

Khabarovsk

Novosibirsk

Krasnoyarsk

Lake Baykal

Novokuznetsk

Angarsk

• Chita

Barnaul

Sayan Mts

Irkutsk

Ulan Ude

Altai Mts

• **Vladivostok**

Trans-Siberian Railway This railway, connecting Moscow in European Russia to Vladivostok on the Pacific Ocean coast, runs across southern Siberia. It is nearly 9,300 km (5,779 miles) long. The journey takes 6 days, 12 hours and 45 minutes to complete.

Volcanoes dot the Kamchatka peninsula, a large area, about the size of Japan, in northeastern Russia. Kamchatka forms part of the Pacific 'ring of fire', a region of active volcanoes and earthquakes that extends around the Pacific Ocean.

MEDITERRANEAN ASIA

At the eastern end of the Mediterranean Sea lies a group of six Asian countries. The largest is Turkey, a small part of which lies in Europe, west of the waterway linking the Mediterranean and Black seas. Turkey is a largely mountainous country with a mild, rainy climate. Cyprus and Lebanon have pleasant sunny climates, but hot deserts cover much of Israel, Jordan and Syria.

Israel was founded as a Jewish state in the ancient region of Palestine in 1948, but it has had to fight for its existence against its Arab neighbours in wars in 1948-9, 1956, 1967 and 1973. In 1967 it gained large areas from Egypt, Jordan and Syria.

TURKEY

Area: 774,815sq km (299,158sq miles), 97% of which is in Asia
Highest point: Mt Ararat 5,185m (17,011ft)
Population: 63,745,000
Capital: Ankara (pop 2,838,000)
Official language: Turkish
Religion: Islam
Government: Republic
Currency: Turkish lira

CYPRUS

Area: 9,251sq km (3,572sq miles)
Highest point: Mt Olympus 1,952m (6,403ft)
Population: 747,000
Capital: Nicosia (pop 177,000)
Official languages: Greek, Turkish
Religions: Christianity, Islam
Government: Republic
Currency: Cyprus pound

SYRIA

Area: 185,180sq km (71,498sq miles)
Highest point: Mt Hermon 2,814m (9,232ft)
Population: 14,895,000
Capital: Damascus (pop 1,550,000)
Official language: Arabic
Religions: Islam (86%)
Government: Republic
Currency: Syrian pound

LEBANON

Area: 10,400sq km (4,015sq miles)
Highest point: Qurnat as Sawda 3,083m (10,115ft)
Population: 4,416,000
Capital: Beirut (pop 1,100,000)
Official language: Turkish
Religions: Islam (55%), Christianity (37%)
Government: Republic
Currency: Lebanese pound

Earthquakes occur in northern Turkey as the land moves along huge faults (cracks) in the earth's crust. At least 13,000 people died in 1999 when an earthquake struck the area near Izmit in northwestern Turkey.

ISRAEL

Area: 21,056sq km (8,130sq miles)
Highest point: Mt Meron 1,208m (3,963ft)
Population: 5,836,000
Capital: Jerusalem (pop 602,000)
Official languages: Hebrew, Arabic
Religions: Judaism (80%), Islam (15%)
Government: Republic
Currency: New sheqel

JORDAN

Area: 97,740sq km (37,738sq miles)
Highest point: Jabal Ramm 1,754m (5,755ft)
Population: 4,437,000
Capital: Amman (pop 963,000)
Official language: Arabic
Religions: Islam (96.5%), Christianity (3.5%)
Government: Monarchy
Currency: Jordan dinar

Jerusalem is a holy city for Christians, Jews and Muslims. From 1949, Israel controlled western Jerusalem and made it their capital in 1950. Eastern Jerusalem was held by Lebanon until Israeli forces captured eastern Jerusalem during the 1967 Arab-Israeli War. Here devout Jews pray at the Wailing Wall, a sacred place of Judaism.

TURKEY IN EUROPE · Zongulд · Istanbul · Adapazari · Izmit · Bursa · Eskisehir · Troy · Edremit · Bergama · Afyon · Menderes · Aydin · Denizil · Isparta · Antalya · Sea of Marmara · Bosporus · Dardanelles · Aegean Sea · Izmir · Lake Egridir · Lake Beysehir · Mediterranean Sea

Map Labels

Black Sea

Samsun
Trabzon
Kars
Corum
Kizil
Ararat 5185m
Ankara
Sivas
Erzincan
Erzurum
Van
Lake Van

T U R K E Y

Lake Tuz
Kayseri
Malatya
Elazig
Taurus Mts
Maras
Seyhan
Diyarbakir
Tigris
Kurdistan

Osmaniye
Gaziantep
Tarsus
Adana
Mersin
Iskenderun
Urfa

Antakya
Aleppo
Euphrates
Khabur

Latakia
Assad Reservoir
Dayr az Zawr

CYPRUS
Nicosia
Olympus 1952m

S Y R I A
Homs
∴ Palmyra

Tripoli
▲ *Qurnat as Sawda 3083m*

Beirut ▣

LEBANON
□ Damascus
Tyre
▲ *Hermon 2814m*

S y r i a n D e s e r t

Haifa
▲ *Meron 1208m*

ISRAEL
Jordan
Tel Aviv-Yafo
Zarqa
West Bank
▣
Jerusalem ▣
Amman

Gaza Strip
Dead Sea

Beersheba
JORDAN

Negev Desert
∴ *Petra*

▲ *Jabal Ramm 1754m*
Elat
Aqaba

0 ___ 100 miles
0 ___ 100 kilometres

Side Panel

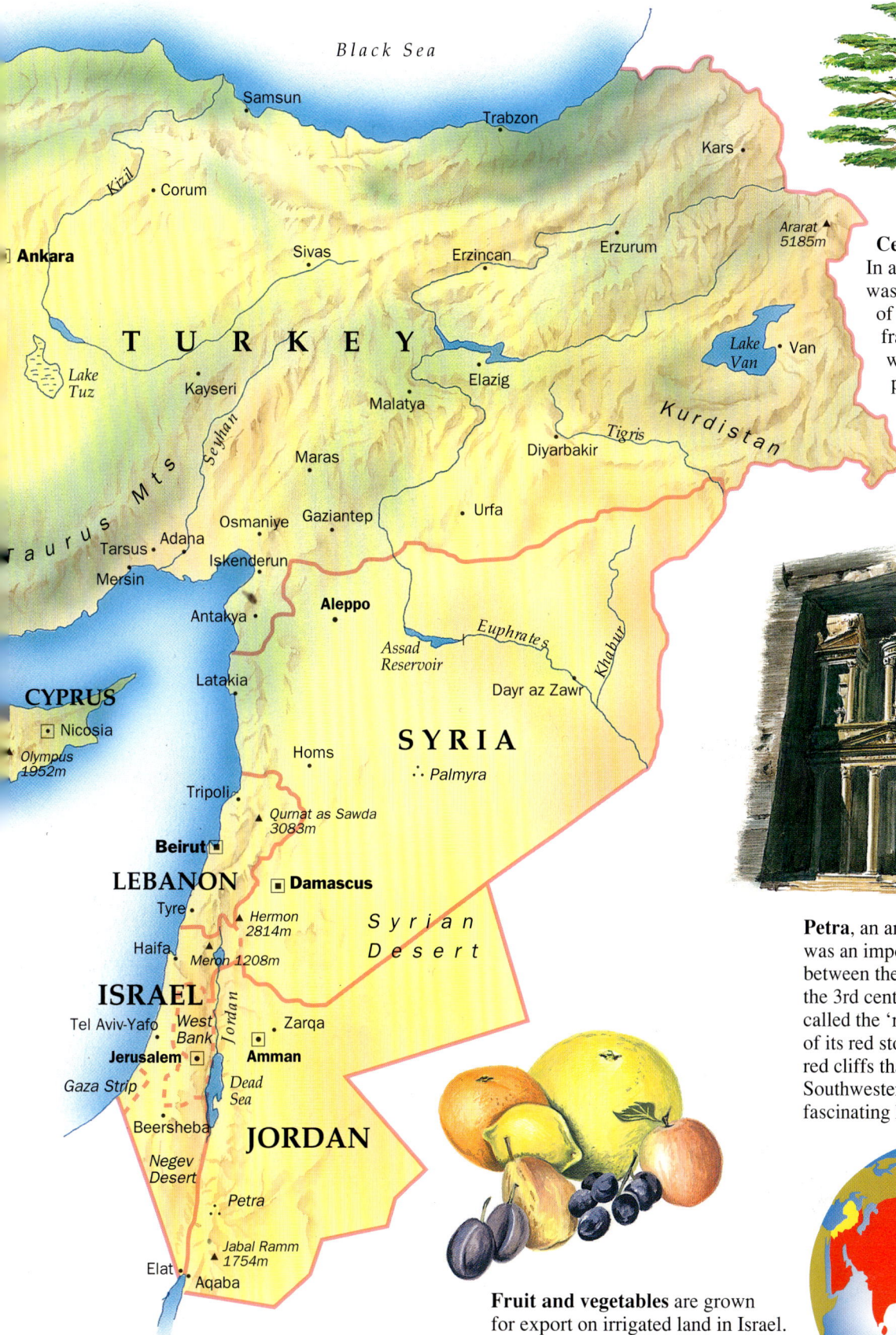

Cedar of Lebanon
In ancient times, Lebanon was famous for its forests of this beautiful tree. Its fragrant, valuable wood was used in building palaces, ships and tombs and most of the forests were cut down. A grove of the trees still survives in the northern mountains.

Petra, an ancient city in Jordan, was an important trading centre between the 5th century BC and the 3rd century AD. Petra is often called the 'rose red' city because of its red stone buildings and the red cliffs that surround it. Southwestern Asia contains many fascinating historic sites.

Fruit and vegetables are grown for export on irrigated land in Israel. But manufacturing accounts for Israel's leading exports. Israel is the most developed and prosperous country in southwestern Asia.

ARABIAN PENINSULA

The Arabian peninsula lies between the Red Sea and The Gulf (also known as the Arabian or Persian Gulf). Hot, thinly populated deserts cover most of the peninsula. Farming is possible only around oases where people can get water from underground rocks. But Bahrain, Oman, Qatar, Saudi Arabia and United Arab Emirates all have rich oil reserves. Yemen is the poorest country in this region.

Mecca in Saudi Arabia was the birthplace of the Prophet Mohammed (?AD 570-632), who founded the religion of Islam. Every year more than a million Muslims from all over the world visit Mecca on a pilgrimage called the hajj.

Arabian oryx This graceful antelope was almost extinct in the Arabian peninsula until some were taken to Phoenix Zoo, Arizona. There, a world herd was established. Animals from this herd have been released in Jordan, Oman and Saudi Arabia.

Muslim women often wear a full-length body veil called a *chador*. This form of clothing is required by strict Muslim teachings, but women in some Muslim countries wear western dress. This woman is wearing a simple scarf called a *hijab*.

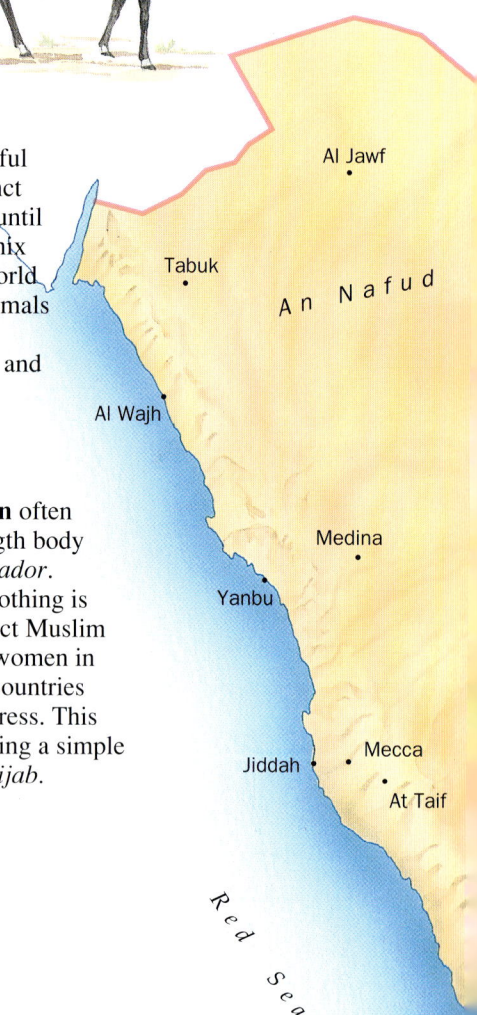

SAUDI ARABIA

Area: 2,149,690sq km (830,000sq miles)
Highest point: 3,139m (10,279ft)
Population: 20,066,000
Capital: Riyadh (pop 1,800,000)
Official language: Arabic
Religions: Islam (97%), Christianity (3%)
Government: Monarchy
Currency: Saudi riyal

YEMEN

Area: 527,968sq km (203,850sq miles)
Highest point: Hadur Shuayb 3,760m (12,336ft)
Population: 16,072,000
Capital: Sana (pop 972,000)
Official language: Arabic
Religions: Islam
Government: Republic
Currency: Yemeni rial

OMAN

Area: 212,457sq km (82,030sq miles)
Highest point: Jabal Ash Sham 3,035m (9,957ft)
Population: 2,256,000
Capital: Muscat (pop 52,000)
Official language: Arabic
Religions: Islam (88%), Hinduism (7%)
Government: Monarchy
Currency: Omani rial

QATAR

Area: 11,000sq km (4,247sq miles)
Population: 721,000
Capital: Doha (pop 339,000)
Official language: Arabic
Religion: Islam
Government: Monarchy
Currency: Qatar riyal

UNITED ARAB EMIRATES

Area: 83,600sq km (32,278sq miles)
Highest point: Jabal Yibir 1,527m (5,010ft)
Population: 2,580,000
Capital: Abu Dhabi (pop 363,000)
Official language: Arabic
Religion: Islam (96%)
Government: Federation of seven emirates
Currency: UAE dirham

BAHRAIN

Area: 694sq km (268sq miles)
Population: 620,000
Capital: Manama (pop 140,000)
Official language: Arabic
Religion: Islam
Government: Monarchy
Currency: Bahrain dinar

Al Jawf

Tabuk

An Nafud

Al Wajh

Medina

Yanbu

Jiddah

Mecca

At Taif

Red Sea

Rub al Khali This bleak desert lies mainly in southern Saudi Arabia and also in Yemen. It is often called the 'Empty Quarter' because it contains the world's largest expanse of sand. Plants are almost non-existent, growing only at oases.

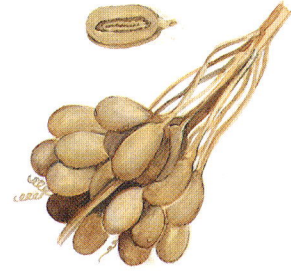

Dates are the nutritious fruits of the date palm, the commonest tree in the Arabian peninsula. The tree trunks are used in building and the leaves are used to make baskets and mats. Dates have been an important food in southwestern Asia for at least 5,000 years.

Camels can travel long distances without having to drink water. They are often called the 'ships of the desert' because they were the traditional means of transporting people and goods across deserts.

The Gulf

Hafar

Buraydah

Damman **BAHRAIN**
Manama

Strait of Hormuz

QATAR
Al Hufuf
Doha

Sharjah
Dubai
Jabal Yibir
1527m

Gulf of Oman

Riyadh

Haradh
UNITED ARAB EMIRATES

Abu Dhabi

Al Khaburah
Muscat

SAUDI ARABIA

Jabal Ash Sham
3035m

R u b   a l   K h a l i

(Empty Quarter)

OMAN

Al' Masira

D h u f a r

A r a b i a n   S e a

'139m
bha

Salalah

H a d h r a m a u t

Sana
YEMEN
Hadur Shuayb 3760m

Al Hudaydah
Zabid
Al Mukalla
Taiz
Mocha
Aden

0	200 miles
0	200 kilometres

Oil tankers transport oil from the Gulf region all around the world. Saudi Arabia is the largest producer and exporter of oil and it has the world's largest known reserves. Money from oil sales has been used to develop industries and welfare services in the Arabian peninsula.

IRAQ, IRAN AND KUWAIT

Iraq contains large deserts but also has a fertile region called Mesopotamia. Mesopotamia means 'the land between the rivers'. The rivers are the Tigris and Euphrates, which rise in Turkey and flow across Iraq. Mesopotamia was the place where Sumer, the oldest known civilization, developed. Later civilizations in Mesopotamia included those of Assyria and Babylon. Iran (formerly Persia) also has many magnificent historic sites, including the ancient city of Persepolis, which was destroyed by Alexander the Great.

Since the 1980s, these oil-rich, Muslim countries have been at war. Iran and Iraq fought between 1980 and 1988. Then, in 1990, Iraq invaded Kuwait. In 1991, an Allied force led by the United States and supported by Britain, Egypt, France, Saudi Arabia and Syria drove Iraqi troops out of Kuwait.

IRAQ

Area: 438,317sq km (169,235sq miles)
Highest point: 3,609m (11,480ft) in Zagros Mts
Population: 21,847,000
Capital and largest city: Baghdad (pop 4,478,000)
Other large cities: Mosul (664,000)
Irbil (486,000)
Official language: Arabic
Religions: Islam (97%), Christianity (3%)
Government: Republic
Currency: Iraqi dinar

IRAN

Area: 1,633,188sq km (642,161sq miles)
Highest point: Mt Damavand 5,604m (18,386ft)
Population: 60,929,000
Capital and largest city: Tehran (pop 6,750,000)
Other large cities: Mashhad (1,964,000)
Esfahan (1,220,000)
Tabriz (1,166,000)
Official language: Farsi (Persian)
Religions: Islam (99%)
Government: Islamic republic
Currency: Iranian rial

KUWAIT

Area: 17,818sq km (6,880sq miles)
Population: 1,809,000
Capital: Kuwait (pop 29,000)
Official language: Arabic
Religions: Islam (95%)
Government: Monarchy
Currency: Kuwait dinar

Kurds are a people who live in mountainous regions in Armenia, Iran, Iraq, Syria and Turkey. Many Kurds want to create their own country. In the 1980s and 1990s, fighting broke out between Kurdish nationalists and government forces in eastern Turkey and northern Iraq.

Ur was a city in ancient Sumer, identified in the Bible as the home of Abraham. The people of Sumer built temples that stood on the top of pyramid-like structures, called *ziggurats*.

Persian carpets are world famous for their beauty. Craft industries are important in Iran. Other products made by hand include glassware, leather, pottery and metal goods, such as trays and tea services.

Scale:
0 — 200 miles
0 — 200 kilometres

Caspian Sea

Gorgan

Elburz Mts

Mashhad

Tehran

Damavand 5604m

Rey

Dasht-e Kavir

Qom

Arak

Kashan

I R A N

Dasht-e Lut

Esfahan

Yazd

Kerman

Persepolis

Shiraz

Zahedan

Bam

Bushehr

Bandar Abbas

The Gulf

Strait of Hormuz

Chah Bahar

Tehran, the capital of Iran, stands at the foot of the Elburz Mountains. This busy industrial city has universities and museums that exhibit treasures from the region's earlier civilizations. This is the Shayhad monument.

Ayatollah Khomeini (1900?-89) led the revolution in 1979 that overthrew the shah (king) of Iran and turned the country into an Islamic republic. Iran's laws are now based closely on the teachings of Islam.

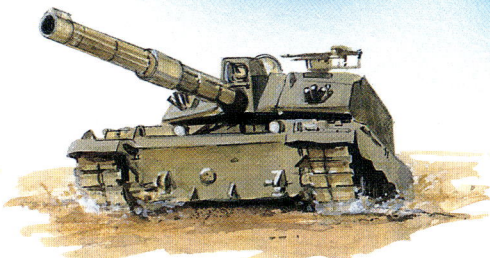

Tanks are a familiar sight in southwestern Asia. In the last 60 years, wars have led neighbouring governments to spend huge amounts of money on military equipment and weapons. Military service is compulsory in both Iran and Iraq.

Kuwait is an oil-rich country at the head of the Gulf. The invasion of Kuwait by Iraq in 1990 and the 1991 Gulf War caused pollution on a huge scale and great damage to Kuwait's oilfields and industrial areas.

CENTRAL ASIA

The five countries of Central Asia were once part of the Soviet Union. They became independent in 1991, when the Soviet Union split up. Kazakhstan, the world's ninth largest country, lies mainly in Asia, though a small area in the west lies in Europe.

Central Asia contains mountains, deserts, huge lakes and vast grassy plains called steppes. Attempts to develop the land have created environmental problems. Much of the river water that once flowed into the Aral Sea, for example, is now used by farmers and the huge lake has shrunk. Areas that were once fishing grounds are now desert.

KAZAKHSTAN

Area: 2,717,000sq km (1,049,040sq miles), 4% of which is in Europe
Highest point: Mt Teneri 6,398m (20,991ft)
Population: 15,801,000
Capital: Astana (formerly Aqmola, Tselinograd)
Official language: Kazak
Religions: Islam (47%), Christianity (10%)
Government: Republic
Currency: Tenge

UZBEKISTAN

Area: 447,400sq km (172,742sq miles)
Highest point: 4,643m (15,233ft) in the southeast
Population: 23,667,000
Capital: Tashkent (pop 2,107,000)
Official language: Uzbek
Religions: Islam (88%)
Government: Republic
Currency: Som

TURKMENISTAN

Area: 488,100sq km (188,546sq miles)
Highest point: Kugitangtau 3,137m (10,292ft)
Population: 4,658,000
Capital: Ashgabat (pop 416,000)
Official language: Turkmen
Religions: Islam (87%)
Government: Republic
Currency: Manat

TAJIKISTAN

Area: 145,100sq km (56,023sq miles)
Highest point: Communism Peak 7,495m (24,590ft)
Population: 6,017,000
Capital: Dushanbe (pop 582,000)
Official language: Tajik
Religions: Islam (85%)
Government: Republic
Currency: Tajik ruble

KYRGYZSTAN

Area: 198,500sq km (76,641sq miles)
Highest point: Peak Pobedy 7,439m (24,406ft)
Population: 4,635,000
Capital: Bishkek (pop 631,000)
Official language: Kyrgyz
Religions: Islam (70%)
Government: Republic
Currency: Som

Cotton is a major crop throughout Central Asia and agriculture is the main activity. The governments of these former Communist countries have been working since 1991 to introduce private ownership of the land and industries.

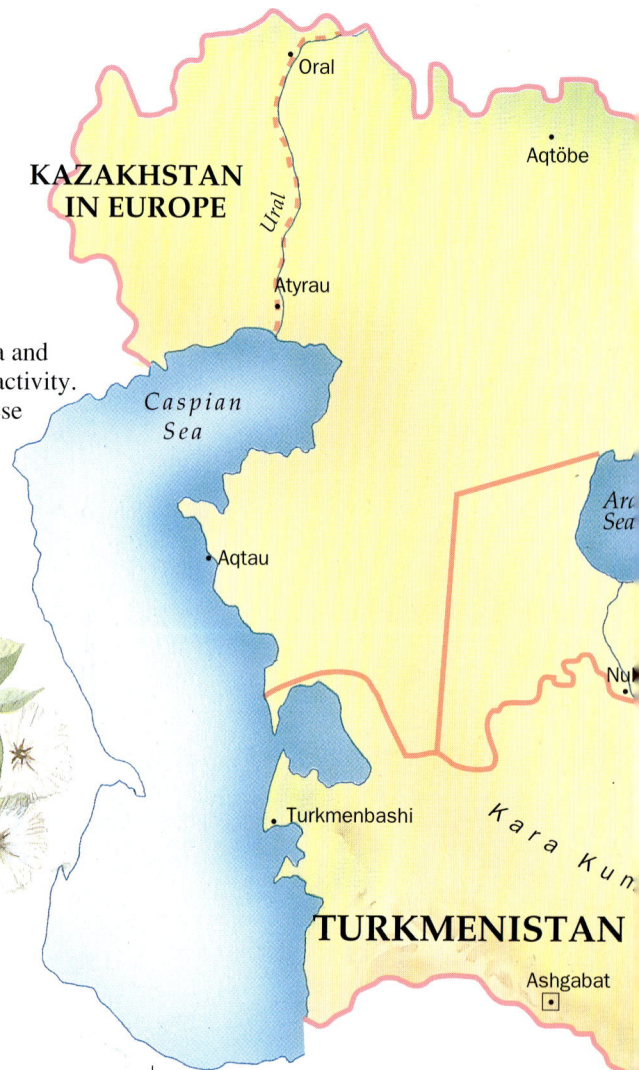

KAZAKHSTAN IN EUROPE

Oral

Aqtöbe

Ural

Atyrau

Caspian Sea

Aqtau

Ara Sea

Nu

Turkmenbashi

Kara Kum

TURKMENISTAN

Ashgabat

0   100 miles
0   100 kilometres

Aral Sea This saltwater lake on the border between Uzbekistan and Kazakhstan has lost 75 per cent of its volume since 1960. Much of the river water that supplied it is now used to irrigate cotton fields. The local fishing industry has been destroyed, with fishing boats left high and dry.

Deserts cover much of Turkmenistan, Uzbekistan and southern Kazakhstan. Northern Kazakhstan contains high plains covered by dry grassland, or steppe. Farmers on horseback look after their cattle and sheep.

Petropavl

Qostanay

Irtysh

Pavlodar

Astana

Semey

Öskemen

Lake Zaysan

Qaraghandy

K A Z A K H S T A N

Baykonur · · Zhezqazghan

ral

Lake Balkhash

Syrdarya

Teneri 6398m

Almaty

Peak Pobedy 7439m

Kyzyl Kum

Zhambyl

Shymkent

Bishkek

KYRGYZSTAN

UZBEKISTAN

Namangan

Tashkent

Andijon

Nawoiy

Bukhara

Samarkand

Communism Peak 7495m

TAJIKISTAN

Amudarya

4643m **Dushanbe**

Pamirs

Kugitangtau 3137m

Baykonur in Kazakhstan was the space centre for the former Soviet Union. Since the Soviet Union was dissolved in 1991, Russia has paid Kazakhstan for use of the site. The first manned orbital flight in 1961 was launched from Baykonur.

Samarkand, in Uzbekistan, was once the capital of the empire of the Mongol emperor Timur (or Tamerlaine). The city has beautiful mosques and other fine buildings, many decorated with mosaics. Islam is the chief religion in Central Asia.

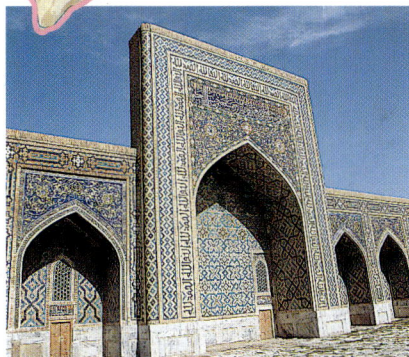

AFGHANISTAN AND PAKISTAN

Landlocked Afghanistan is one of the world's poorest countries. Highlands and mountains cover most of the land. Since Afghanistan became a republic in 1973, it has suffered from droughts, famine and civil war. By the end of the century, most of the country had come under the rule of a strict Muslim group, called the Taleban.

Pakistan has high mountains, but also fertile plains drained by the Indus River and its tributaries. Pakistan became an independent country in 1947, when it broke away from British India. It remains in dispute with India over the region called Kashmir. Fighting along the border between Pakistan and India has occurred several times.

AFGHANISTAN

Area: 652,090sq km (251,773sq miles)
Highest point: Nowshak, in the Hindu Kush, 7,485m (24,557ft)
Population: 24,965,000
Capital and largest city: Kabul (pop 700,000)
Other large cities: Kandahar (225,000)
Herat (177,000)
Mazar-e-Sharif (130,000)
Jalalabad (55,000)
Official languages: Pashto, Dari (Persian)
Religion: Islam
Government: Islamic emirate
Currency: Afghani

PAKISTAN

Area: 796,095sq km (307,374sq miles)
Highest point: K2 8,611m (28,250ft)
Population: 128,457,000
Capital: Islamabad (pop 204,000)
Largest cities: Karachi (5,208,000)
Lahore (2,953,000)
Hyderabad (1,151,000)
Gujranwala (1,125,000)
Faisalabad (1,104,000)
Rawalpindi (795,000)
Official language: Urdu
Religions: Islam (95%), Christianity (2%), Hinduism (2%)
Government: Military regime
Currency: Pakistan rupee

Muslims pray five times a day, at dawn, noon, in the afternoon and evening, and finally at nightfall. When they pray, they always face Mecca, the birthplace of the Prophet Mohammed. Afghanistan and Pakistan are both Islamic states.

Fruits of many kinds are grown in Afghanistan and Pakistan. The economies of both countries depend on agriculture. Wheat is their chief food crop. Many farmers raise goats and sheep. Manufacturing is increasing in Pakistan.

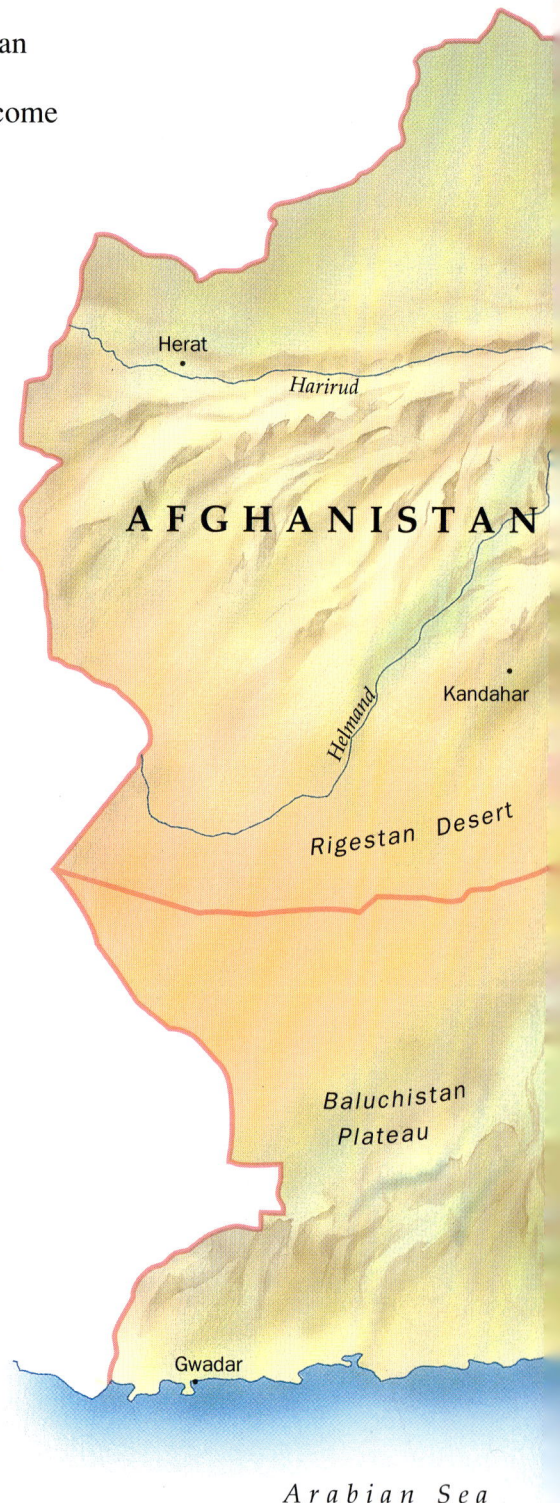

Herat

Harirud

A F G H A N I S T A N

Helmand

Kandahar

Rigestan Desert

Baluchistan Plateau

Gwadar

Arabian Sea

| 0 | | 100 miles |
| 0 | | 100 kilometres |

PAKISTAN

Amudarya

Feyzabad

azar-e-Sharif

Baghlan

Nowshak
7485m

Hindu Kush

Chariker

Karakoram Mts

K2
8611m

Kashmir

Indus

Kabul

Kabul

Jalalabad

Khyber Pass

Mardan

Ghazni

Peshawar

Islamabad

Rawalpindi

Gujrat

Bannu

Jhelum

Sialkot

Sargodha

Gujranwala

Faisalabad

Lahore

Ravi

Punjab

Multan

Chenab

Sutlej

Quetta

Bahawalpur

PAKISTAN

Indus

Shikarpur

Sukkur

Mohenjo Daro

Mirpur Khas

Hyderabad

Karachi

The ownership of
this area is in dispute
between Pakistan
and India

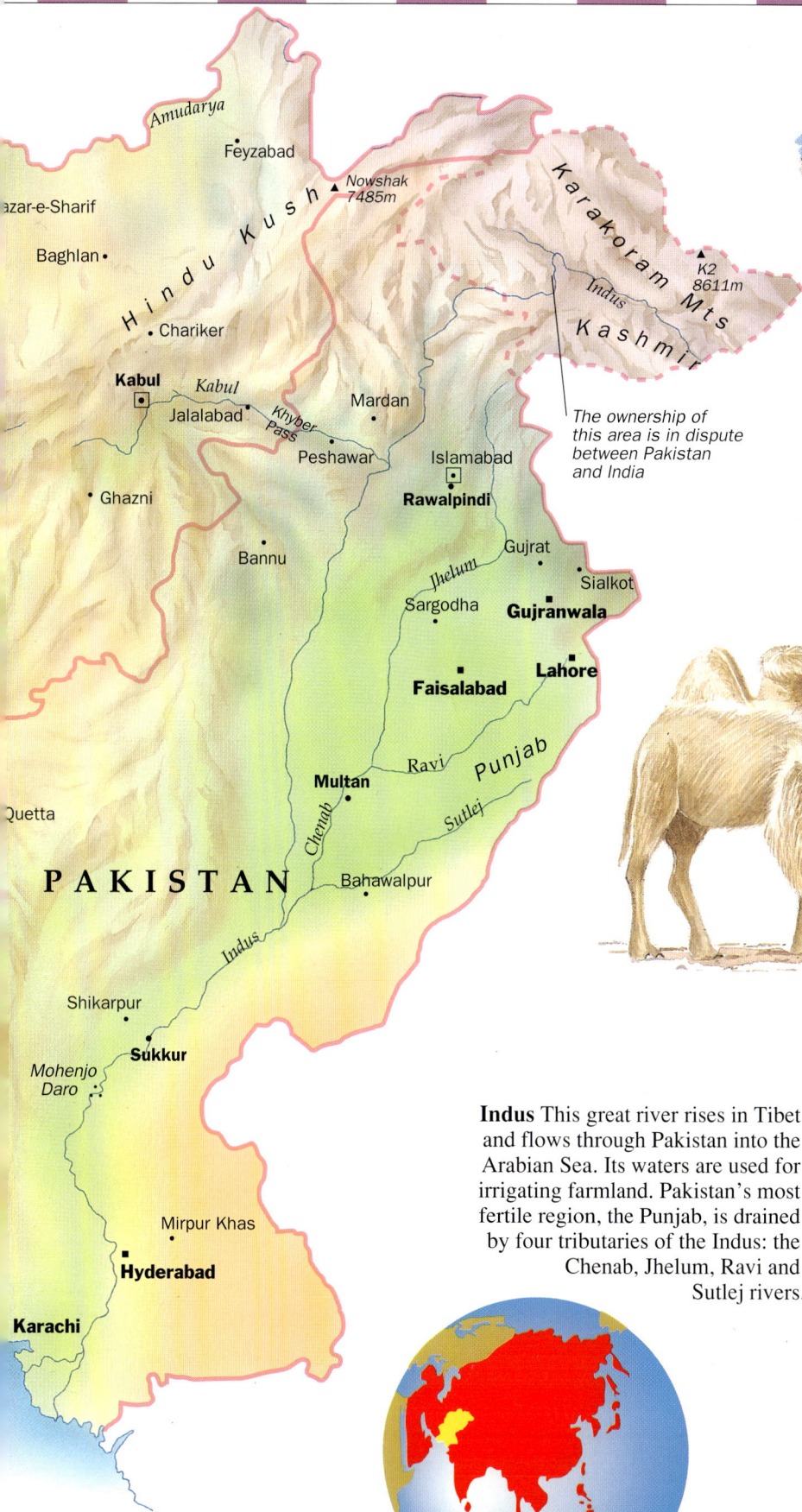

Kashmir is an area that lies on the border between Pakistan and India. Each of the countries claims Kashmir. The present border is the cease-fire line that was established after heavy fighting broke out between Pakistan and India in 1971.

Bactrian camels are sturdy animals with two humps, unlike the Arabian camel, or dromedary, which has only one hump. Bactrian camels are found in the cold regions of eastern and central Asia, where they are important beasts of burden.

Indus This great river rises in Tibet and flows through Pakistan into the Arabian Sea. Its waters are used for irrigating farmland. Pakistan's most fertile region, the Punjab, is drained by four tributaries of the Indus: the Chenab, Jhelum, Ravi and Sutlej rivers.

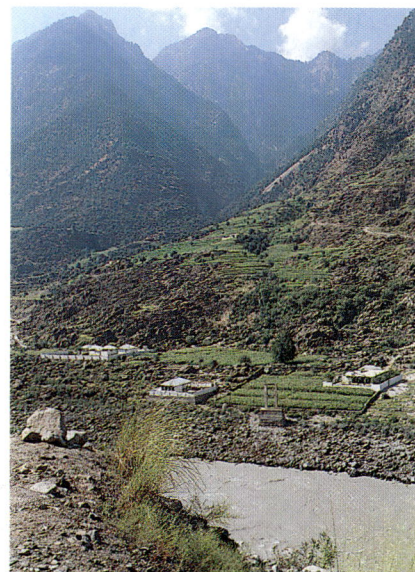

INDIAN SUBCONTINENT

India is the world's seventh largest country, but in population it ranks second only to China. Northern India is mountainous, and long rivers, including the Ganges, flow down from the mountains and across the fertile plains to the south of the mountains. South India is a tableland called the Deccan. India became independent from Britain in 1947.

The Indian subcontinent also includes Bhutan and Nepal, two mountainous countries in the Himalaya region, and the beautiful island country of Sri Lanka (formerly called Ceylon) which lies off the southern tip of India. The Maldives is an island nation lying to the southwest of southern India.

INDIA

Area: 3,287,590sq km (1,269,346sq miles)
Highest point: Kanchenjunga 8,598m (28,208ft)
Population: 962,378,000
Capital: New Delhi (pop 301,000)
Largest cities: Mumbai (formerly Bombay, 9,926,000)
Delhi (7,207,000)
Calcutta (Kolkata, 4,400,000)
Chennai (formerly Madras, 3,841,000)
Official languages: Hindi, English
Religions: Hinduism (81%), Islam (12%), Christianity (2%), other (5%)
Government: Federal republic
Currency: Indian rupee

SRI LANKA

Area: 65,610sq km (25,332sq miles)
Highest point: Pidurutalagala 2,524m (8,281ft)
Population: 18,552,000
Capital: Colombo (pop 615,000)
Official languages: Sinhala, Tamil
Religions: Buddhism (69%), Hinduism (15%), Islam (7%), Christianity (8%)
Government: Republic
Currency: Sri Lanka rupee

NEPAL

Area: 147,181sq km (56,827sq miles)
Highest point: Mt Everest 8,848m (29,029ft)
Population: 22,321,000
Capital: Katmandu (pop 535,000)
Other large cities: Lalitapur (190,000)
Official language: Nepali
Religions: Hinduism (86%), Buddhism (8%)
Government: Monarchy
Currency: Nepalese rupee

MALDIVES

Area: 298sq km (115sq miles)
Highest point: 24m (80ft) on Wilingili Island west of Male
Population: 256,000
Capital: Male (pop 63,000)
Official language: Divehi
Religion: Islam
Government: Republic
Currency: Maldivian rufiyaa

BHUTAN

Area: 47,000sq km (18,147sq miles)
Highest point: Kula Kangri 7,554m (24,783ft)
Population: 737,000
Capital: Thimphu (pop 30,000)
Official language: Dzongkha
Religions: Buddhism (75%), Hinduism (25%)
Government: Monarchy
Currency: Ngultrum

0   200 miles
0   200 kilometres

Srinagar   Leh
Jammu
Amritsar
Jullundur   Chandigarh
Ludhiana   Dehra Dun
Meerut
Delhi
Bikaner   New Delhi   Aligarh   Bareill
Jaipur   Agra   Luckno
Ajmer   Kanpur
Jodhpur   Gwalior
Kota
Great Indian (Thar) Desert
Bhopal
Ahmadabad   Ujjain
Indore
Jamnagar   Rajkot   Vadodara   *Narmada*
Bhavnagar   Nagpur
Surat
Aurangabad   I N D I A
Arabian Sea
Mumbai   *Godavari*
Pune   Warang
Sholapur
Hyderabad
Deccan Plateau
Goa
Western Ghats
Bangalore   Chen
Mangalore   Mysore
Salem
Kozhikode   Tiruchchirappa
Coimbatore
Cochin   Madurai
Tirunelveli
Thiruvananthapuram
MALDIVES   *INDIAN OCEAN*
Male

Himalayas The Himalayas is a range of mountains that borders the Indian subcontinent in the north. It contains the world's highest peak, Mount Everest, which stands on the border between Nepal and China. Bhutan also contains part of the Himalayas.

NEPAL

Katmandu

Lalitapur

Everest 8848m

Kanchenjunga 8598m

Darjiling

Kula Kangri 7554m

BHUTAN

Thimphu

Brahmaputra

Guwahati

Gorakhpur

Faizabad

Patna

Bhagalpur

ahabad

Ganges

Imphal

Varanasi

Asanol

Ranchi

Jamshedpur

Calcutta

Haora

Bilaspur

Raipur

Cuttack

Bay of Bengal

Vishakhapatnam

jayawada

na

SRI LANKA

Pidurutalagala 2524m

olombo

Mohandas Gandhi (1869-1948) was a great political and spiritual leader in India. People called him the *Mahatma*, a title meaning 'Great Soul'. Gandhi helped to free India from Britain, using non-violent resistance to oppose the government. He was assassinated in 1948.

Hindu gods are believed by most Hindus to be different aspects of the one god Brahman. Statues like this one are placed in temples and homes. Hindu beliefs and practices vary throughout India and worshippers celebrate many festivals.

Taj Mahal One of the world's most famous and beautiful buildings, the Taj Mahal is in Agra, northwestern India. It was built between 1630 and 1650 by an Indian ruler, Shah Jehan, as a tomb for his beloved wife, Mumtaz Mahal.

Tea India is the world's leading tea producer, followed by China and Sri Lanka. India's chief food crops are rice and wheat. India has more cattle than any other country but Hindus do not eat meat. They regard cattle as sacred animals.

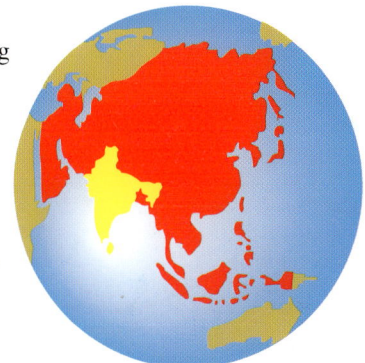

CHINA, MONGOLIA AND TAIWAN

China is the world's third largest country after Russia and Canada. But in population it ranks first. China includes Hong Kong, a former British territory that was returned to China in 1997, and Macau, a former Portuguese territory that was returned in 1999. China also claims the island of Taiwan, but the Taiwanese do not want to be ruled by the Communist government of China.

China became a Communist country in 1949. But since the late 1970s it has been changing. The government has encouraged private ownership of land and invited foreign companies to invest in new industries in eastern China.

Giant panda This endangered animal is the symbol used by the World Wide Fund for Nature. In the wild, pandas are found in only a few remaining bamboo forests on mountain slopes in western and southwestern China. The giant panda is protected by law.

CHINA

Area: 9,562,074sq km (3,691,938sq miles)
Highest point: Mt Everest 8,848m (29,029ft)
Population: 1,206,201,000
Capital: Beijing (pop 6,560,000)
Other large cities: Shanghai (8,760,000)
Tianjin (4,970,000)
Shenyang (3,860,000)
Wuhan (3,860,000)
Official language: Mandarin Chinese
Religions: Chinese folk religions (20%), Buddhism (8%), Christianity (6%)
Government: People's republic
Currency: Renminbi (yuan)

MONGOLIA

Area: 1,566,500sq km (604,829sq miles)
Highest point: 4,362m (14,311ft) in the Altai Mts
Population: 2,542,000
Capital: Ulan Bator (pop 627,000)
Official language: Khalkha Mongolian
Religions: Lamaism, a kind of Buddhism, (96%), Islam (4%)
Government: Republic
Currency: Tugrik

TAIWAN

Area: 35,980sq km (13,892sq miles)
Highest point: Tu Shan 3,997m (13,113ft)
Population: 21,424,000
Capital: Taipei (pop 2,596,000)
Official language: Mandarin Chinese
Religions: Traditional beliefs combining Buddhism, Confucianism and Taoism
Government: Republic
Currency: New Taiwan dollar

Mao Zedong (1893-1976) led the struggle to make China a Communist country. From 1949 he was a powerful ruler whose writings influenced many people around the world. After his death, China's leaders began a series of reforms.

Altay

Yining

Tian Shan

Urümqi

Aksu

Kashi

Taklimakan Desert

C H

Hotan

Altun Mts

Kunlun Mts

Tibetan Plateau

Himalayas

Lhasa

Everest
8848m

0		500 miles

0		500 kilometres

Guilin in southeastern China has some spectacular scenery. Natural crags of limestone rock rise above green rice fields. The rocks have sometimes been likened to dragons' teeth. In Chinese mythology, dragons are friendly not fearsome creatures.

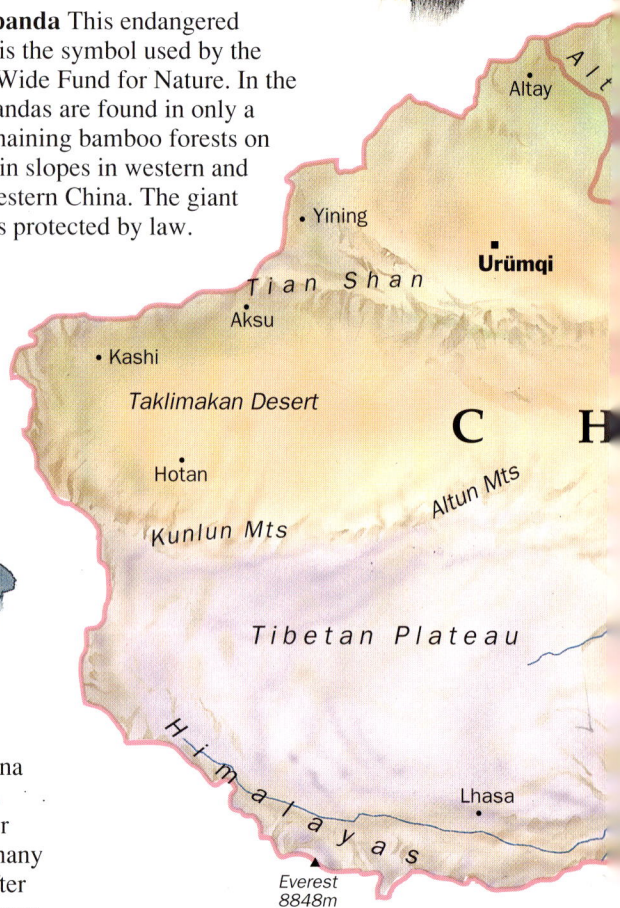

Mongolian nomads live in tents made of felt, called yurts. Mongolia was a Communist country between 1924 and 1990 when free elections were held. Under Communism, many nomads were resettled in permanent settlements.

Shipbuilding is a leading industry in Taiwan, which has become a major industrial centre. It also produces electronic goods. China regards Taiwan as one of its provinces, but the Taiwanese have their own government.

Hong Kong was a British dependency until 1997 when it became a Special Administrative Region of China. Hong Kong is a major financial and industrial centre and China agreed that it should continue its free enterprise system for at least 50 years.

Erdenet

Ulan Bator

MONGOLIA

4362m

Gobi Desert

Ats

INA

Qiqihar

Hegang

Harbin

Jixi

Changchun

Jilin

Shenyang

Fushun

Jinzhou

Anshan

Boatou

Datong

Great Wall

Beijing

Tangshan

Huang He

Taiyuan

Tianjin

Dalian

Shijiazhuang

Zibo

Lanzhou

Handan

Jinan

Qingdao

Yellow Sea

Luoyang

Grand Canal

Zhengzhou

Xj'an

Huainan

Nanjing

Chengdu

Chang Jiang (Yangtze)

Wuhan

Hefei

Shanghai

Chongqing

Hangzhou

Ningbo

Linhai

Zhaotong

Nanchang

Changsha

East China Sea

Guiyang

Fuzhou

Baoshan

Guilin

Taipei

Kunming

Liuzhou

TAIWAN

Mekong

Xi Jiang

Guangzhou

Shantou

Tu Shan 3997m

Macau

Hong Kong

Kaohsiung

Haikou

South China Sea

Hainan

Amur

KOREAN PENINSULA

The Korean peninsula juts out from northeastern China, separating the Yellow Sea to the west from the Sea of Japan to the east. From 1910 the Korean peninsula was a Japanese colony. But in 1945, at the end of World War II, Russian troops occupied the northern part of the peninsula, while American forces occupied the south.

This division led to the creation of Communist North Korea and non-Communist South Korea. The two countries fought against each other between 1950 and 1953, when the present boundary was agreed. Tension between them continued throughout the second half of the 20th century. North Korea is less developed than South Korea, which is a fast-growing industrial country.

Kim Il Sung (1912-94) headed the government of North Korea, ruling as a dictator from 1948, when the Communist Democratic People's Republic was established, until his death in 1994. He was succeeded by his son, Kim Jong Il.

SOUTH KOREA

Area: 99,274sq km (38,330sq miles)
Highest point: Halla 1,950m (6,398ft)
Population: 45,991,000
Capital and largest city: Seoul (pop 10,229,000)
Other large cities: Pusan (3,814,000)
Taegu (2,449,000)
Inchon (2,308,000)
Taejon (1,272,000)
Official language: Korean
Religions: Christianity (26%), Buddhism (23%)
Government: Republic
Currency: Won

NORTH KOREA

Area: 120,538sq km (46,540sq miles)
Highest point: Paektu 2,744m (9,003ft)
Population: 22,893,000
Capital and largest city: Pyongyang (pop 2,639,000)
Other large cities: Hamhung (775,000)
Chongjin (754,000)
Nampo (691,000)
Official language: Korean
Religions: Traditional beliefs, Chondogyo
Government: People's republic
Currency: Won

Seoul, the capital of South Korea, is one of the world's largest cities. Modern skyscrapers show just how fast South Korea has developed since the 1950s. But the city still has many beautiful old buildings.

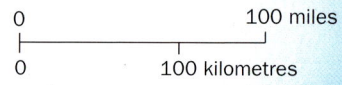

Cars and computers are among the many goods exported by South Korea. The country also ranks among the world's top ten producers of cement, commercial vehicles, steel, televisions and tyres.

NORTH

Sinuiju
Anju
Taedong

Pyongyang
Nampo

Kaesong
Haeju
Inchon

Yellow Sea

0   100 miles
0   100 kilometres

Cheju

Buddhism has long been an important religion in South Korea. In North Korea, the Communist government has discouraged religious worship and around two-thirds of the people say they have no religion.

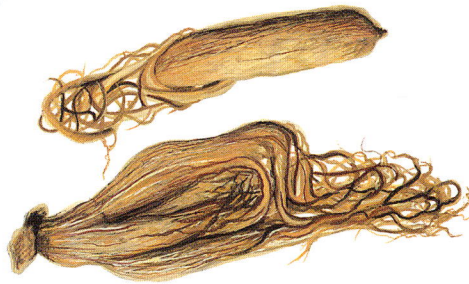

Ginseng is a herb increasingly cultivated in the Korean peninsula and China for export. Many people believe that it can cure a variety of illnesses. It is used in hair tonics, soft drinks, shampoos, skin creams and other 'health' products.

North and South Korea are separated by a Demilitarized Zone, with guards patrolling the frontier. In 1991 the two countries became members of the United Nations. They signed an agreement not to use force against each other, but tension between them continued.

Manufacturing is the most valuable activity in South Korea. The country ranks second only to Japan in shipbuilding. South Korea suffered a slump in 1997-8, but by the turn of the century the economy was reviving.

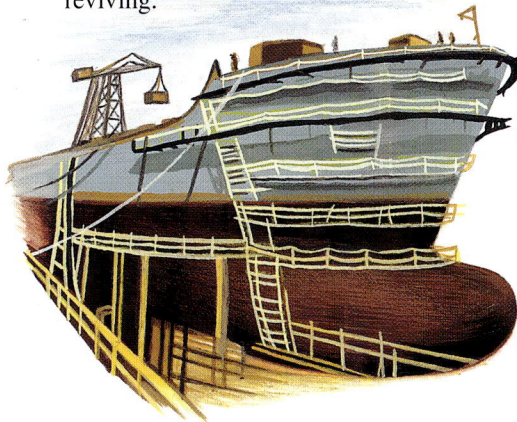

▲ Paektu
2744m

Chongjin

Kimchaek

OREA

Hamhung

Sea of
Japan

Wonsan

Chunchon

Kangnung

eoul

Han

Wonju

onan

SOUTH KOREA

Taejon

Taegu

san

Chonju

Ulsan

Masan

Pusan

Kwangju

Yosu

alla
950m

JAPAN

Japan consists of four large islands, which together make up 98 per cent of the country, and thousands of tiny islands. Much of the land is mountainous, but most people live on the small, fertile plains around the coast. Japan lies on an unstable part of the earth, called the Pacific 'ring of fire'. The country has more than 150 volcanoes, 60 of which are active, and earthquakes are common.

In 1945, after its defeat in World War II, Japan was in ruins. But it is now the world's second biggest economy after the United States. It imports most of the fuels and materials it needs for its huge industries, which have been successful largely through the hard work and skill of its workers and the use of modern technology.

Sumo is a Japanese form of wrestling in which the wrestler tries to throw his opponent to the ground or force him outside a 4.6-metre (15-ft) circle. Judo, karate and kendo (a form of fencing) are other popular sports in Japan.

JAPAN

Area: 377,801sq km (145,870sq miles)
Highest point: Mount Fuji 3,776m (12,388ft)
Population: 126,091,000
Capital and largest city: Tokyo (pop 11,772,000)
Other large cities: Yokohama (3,307,000)
Osaka (2,602,000)
Nagoya (2,152,000)
Sapporo (1,757,000)
Kyoto (1,463,000)
Kobe (1,424,000)
Official language: Japanese
Religions: Shinto and related religions, including Buddhism (93%)
Government: Monarchy
Currency: Yen

Silkworms are the caterpillars, or larvae, of a moth. They feed on the leaves of the white mulberry tree. When fully grown, the silkworms spin a silken cocoon (outer wrapping) around themselves, which is the source of silk thread. Japan is one of the world's top silk producers.

Emperor Akihito is Japan's head of state. He succeeded his father Hirohito in 1989. Before World War II, the Japanese regarded Hirohito as a god. After the war, new laws made him a constitutional monarch.

Mount Fuji is a dormant (sleeping) volcano that last erupted in 1707-8. The snow-capped mountain, which is also called Fuji-yama, is on the island of Honshu. The Japanese regard it as a sacred mountain.

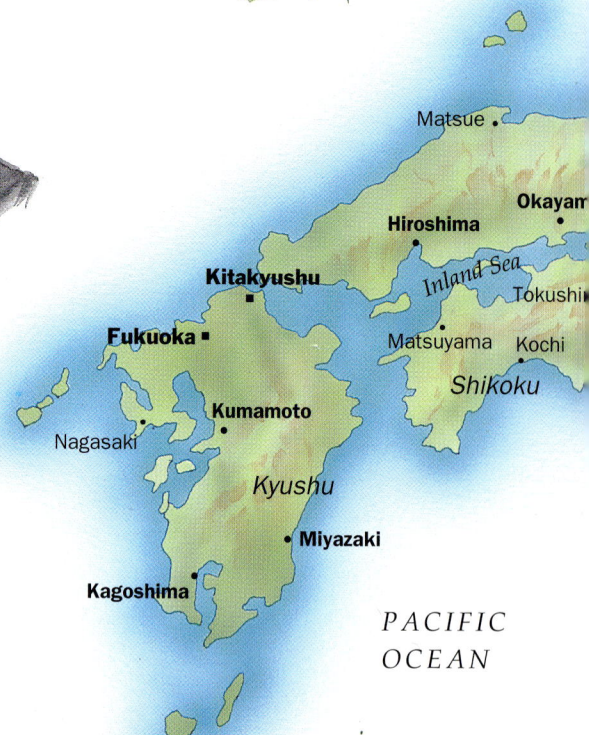

Matsue

Okayam

Hiroshima

Kitakyushu

Fukuoka

Inland Sea

Tokushi

Matsuyama   Kochi

Shikoku

Kumamoto

Nagasaki

Kyushu

Miyazaki

Kagoshima

PACIFIC OCEAN

Fish are an important part of the diet of Japanese people. Because farmland is scarce, Japan once lacked protein-rich foods, such as meat. Now, however, the people eat increasing amounts of meat and dairy products.

Wakkanai

Abashiri

Asahikawa

Hokkaido

Sapporo

Kushiro

Hakodate

North Pacific Ocean

Aomori

Hachinohe

Morioka

Akita

0   100 miles

0   100 kilometres

Sakata

Yamagata

Sendai

Niigata

Fukushima

Sea of Japan

Honshu

Kanazawa

Hitachi

J A P A N

Tokyo

Fuji 3776m

Kawasaki

Kyoto   **Nagoya**

Yokohama

obe

Osaka

Sakai

Hamamatsu

Wakayama

Earthquakes cause great damage. In 1923 an earthquake hit the Tokyo-Yokohama area, killing about 143,000 people. In 1995 another earthquake struck the city of Kobe. More than 5,000 people died.

Calligraphy is the art of beautiful writing. The Japanese and Chinese regard it as an art. Written Japanese uses Chinese characters and Japanese phonetic symbols that represent sounds. Japanese is also written in the Roman alphabet.

髪

Motor cycles are produced in Japanese factories. Japan also leads the world in producing cars and ships, and is a major producer of commercial vehicles and electronic goods, such as computers, radios, personal stereos, telephones and televisions.

Tokyo, the capital of Japan, is one of the world's largest cities. Its tall buildings and busy streets reflect its importance as Japan's chief business centre. But its parks, with their cherry trees, recall traditional Japan.

BANGLADESH, MYANMAR AND THAILAND

Bangladesh was once part of British India. In 1947 it became part of Pakistan and was called East Pakistan. In 1971 East Pakistan broke away and became the independent country of Bangladesh. Bangladesh is a poor but thickly populated country. It is often hit by floods which cause great human suffering.

   Myanmar (formerly Burma) and Thailand are two of the countries in a region called Southeast Asia. Myanmar is another poor country which has been ruled by the military since 1962. Many people have criticized Myanmar's government for its bad human rights record. By contrast, in the second half of the 20th century, Thailand had become one of the wealthier countries in eastern Asia.

BANGLADESH

Area: 143,998sq km (55,598sq miles)
Highest point: Mt Keokradong 1,230m (4,034ft)
Population: 123,633,000
Capital and largest city: Dhaka (pop 6,105,000)
Other large cities: Chittagong (2,040,000)
Official language: Bengali
Religions: Islam (88%), Hinduism (10%)
Government: Republic
Currency: Taka

MYANMAR

Area: 676,578sq km (261,228sq miles)
Highest point: Hkakabo Razi 5,881m (19,296ft)
Population: 43,893,000
Capital and largest city: Yangon (pop 2,513,000)
Other large cities: Mandalay (533,000)
Official language: Burmese
Religions: Buddhism (89%), Christianity (5%), Islam (4%)
Government: Military regime
Currency: Kyat

THAILAND

Area: 513,115sq km (198,115sq miles)
Highest point: Inthanon Mountain 2,595m (8,514ft)
Population: 60,602,000
Capital and largest city: Bangkok (pop 5,620,000)
Official language: Thai
Religions: Buddhism (95%), Islam (4%)
Government: Monarchy
Currency: Baht

Floods are caused in Bangladesh when heavy rains make the rivers overflow. Other floods occur when tropical storms, called cyclones, hit the coast. Strong winds push seawater inland, flooding the flat coastal plains.

Buddhist monks are a familiar sight in Myanmar and Thailand. In Myanmar most boys spend time in their local monastery. Some stay for a few weeks, others for years.

0 ⎯⎯ 200 miles
0 ⎯⎯ 200 kilometres

Hkakabo Razi
5881m
Putao

Myitkyina

Lashio

MYANMAR

Gemstones Myanmar is famous for its fine rubies and sapphires. Thailand also produces a wide range of precious stones, which are used to make beautiful jewellery, though Thailand's most valuable mineral is tin.

Siamese cats originated in Thailand, which was formerly called Siam. These popular cats were once used to guard palaces and temples. Their miaows are loud and persistent enough to attract attention.

Jute is a tough fibre that comes from jute plants. The plants grow best in warm, humid climates and are cultivated. Jute is used to make sacks and cloth. Bangladesh ranks second only to India in the production of jute.

Inthanon
2595m
Chiang-Mai

Mawlamyine

Udon Thani

THAILAND

Khon Kaen

Nakhon
Sawan

Nakhon
Ratchasima

Ubon
Ratchathani

Bangkok, the capital of Thailand, stands on the Chao Phraya river. It is a busy commercial and industrial centre. It also has many beautiful palaces and Buddhist temples, and a busy floating market.

Dawei Thon Buri

Bangkok

Chon Buri

Mergui

Gulf of Thailand

Isthmus of Kra

Surat Thani
Nakhon Si
Thammarat

Phuket

Songkhla

Computer technology plays an important part in the industry and economy of Thailand. Factories produce computers and computer software, and machinery of various kinds is now the country's leading export.

CAMBODIA, LAOS AND VIETNAM

Cambodia, Laos and Vietnam form a region called Indochina. The region was ruled by France until 1954. Vietnam was divided into two parts: Communist North Vietnam and non-Communist South Vietnam. The division of Vietnam led to the Vietnam War (1957-75). Eventually, Vietnam was reunited as a single Communist country called the Socialist Republic of Vietnam.

Cambodia, Laos and Vietnam are poor developing countries that have been badly scarred by war. Most of their people depend on farming for their living. Manufacturing is increasing, especially in Vietnam.

CAMBODIA

Area: 181,035sq km (69,898sq miles)
Highest point: 1,813m (5,948ft) in west-central Cambodia
Population: 10,480,000
Capital and largest city: Phnom Penh (pop 920,000)
Official language: Khmer
Religions: Buddhism (95%), Islam (2%)
Government: Republic
Currency: Riel

LAOS

Area: 236,800sq km (91,429sq miles)
Highest point: Mt Bia 2,817m (9,242ft)
Population: 4,849,000
Capital and largest city: Vientiane (pop 178,000)
Other large cities: Savannakhet (97,000)
Official language: Lao
Religions: Buddhism (58%), local religions (34%)
Government: People's republic
Currency: Kip

VIETNAM

Area: 331,689sq km (128,066sq miles)
Highest point: Fan Si Pan 3,143m (10,312ft)
Population: 76,711,000
Capital: Hanoi (pop 2,155,000)
Largest cities: Ho Chi Minh City (4,322,000) Haiphong (783,000)
Official language: Vietnamese
Religions: Buddhism (67%), Christianity (9%)
Government: Socialist republic
Currency: Dong

Angkor Wat is a huge temple built in northern Cambodia in the 12th century in honour of the Hindu god Vishnu. It is perhaps the finest of the many ancient temples found in Cambodia.

Rice is the main food crop in all of the three countries in Indochina. The rice shoots are planted in the muddy soil in flooded fields. Rice grows well in the warm, humid climates of these countries.

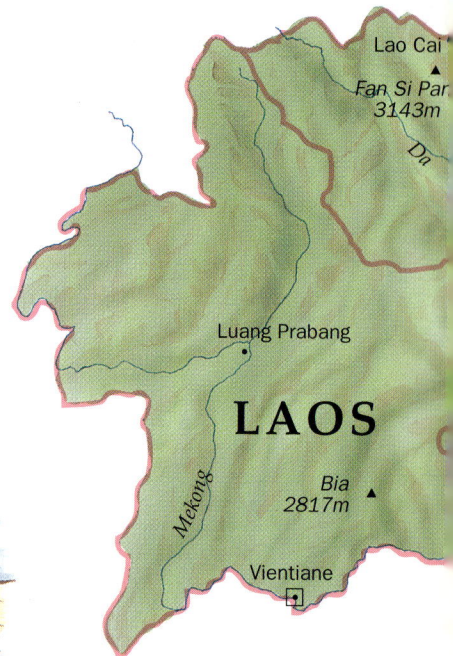

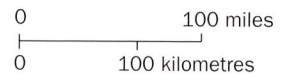

0   100 miles
0   100 kilometres

Gulf of Thailand

Ha Giang

Lang Son

Hanoi

Hoa Binh **Haiphong**

Ninh Binh

VIETNAM

Vinh

South China Sea

Annamite Range

Savannakhet

Mekong

Quang Tri

Hue

Da Nang

Pakse

Qui Nhon

Stung Treng

CAMBODIA

Nha Trang

Kompong Cham

Da Lat

Cam Ranh

hnom Penh   Tay Ninh

Ho Chi Minh City

Mekong

ach Gia   My Tho

Can Tho

Ca Mau

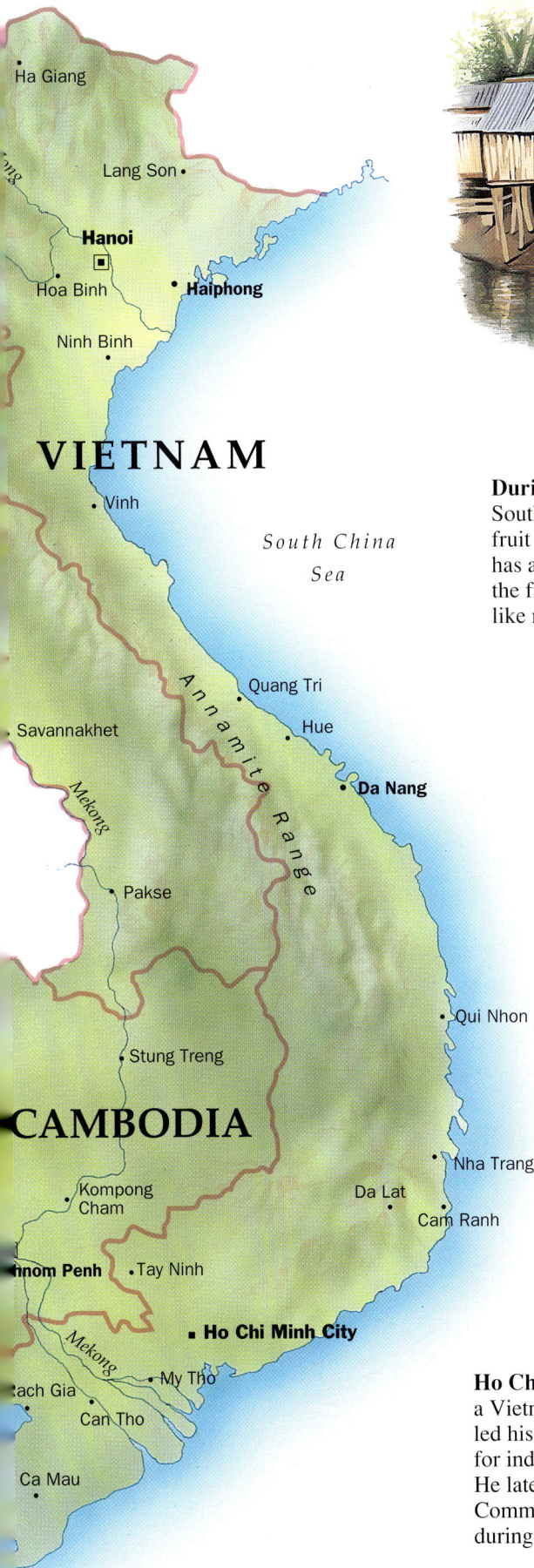

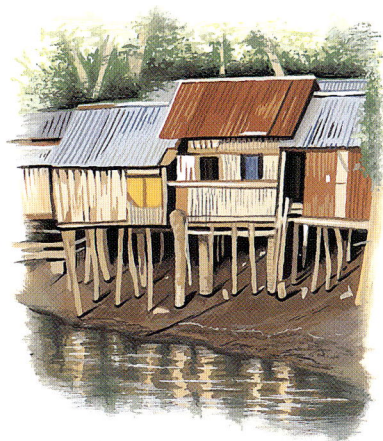

Houses in Indochinese villages are often made of wood or bamboo and built on stilts. This keeps them dry when floods occur. About 80 per cent of the people of Indochina live in the countryside.

Durian is a fruit grown in Southeast Asia. The spherical fruit has a hard shell. The flesh has a pleasant sweet taste, but the fruit has a strong smell, like ripe cheese.

Mekong River
The Mekong, the longest river in Indochina, rises in Tibet. It forms part of the border between Thailand and Laos and then flows across Laos, Cambodia and Vietnam before emptying into the South China Sea near Ho Chi Minh City.

Ho Chi Minh (1890-1969) was a Vietnamese Communist, who led his country in the struggle for independence from France. He later served as president of Communist North Vietnam during the Vietnam War.

MALAYSIA, SINGAPORE AND BRUNEI

Malaysia is a large country. It includes the Malaysian peninsula, which is joined to mainland Asia, and two areas in northern Borneo called Sabah and Sarawak. This hot and rainy country has developed quickly since 1963, when Malaya, a British territory until 1957, agreed to unite with Singapore, Sabah and Sarawak.

Singapore, a small island country which was also once ruled by Britain, withdrew from Malaysia in 1965. It is now one of the most prosperous places in Asia. Brunei, a small country in Borneo, which became independent from Britain in 1984, is also prosperous. Its wealth comes from its rich oil reserves.

Singapore consists of one large island, also called Singapore, and 58 small ones. Its people are highly skilled and hardworking, and have made their country a major industrial centre. Trade and finance are also important.

MALAYSIA

Area: 329,758sq km (127,320sq miles)
Highest point: Mt Kinabalu 4,094m (13,431ft)
Population: 21,667,000
Capital and largest city: Kuala Lumpur (pop 1,145,000)
Other large cities: Ipoh (383,000) Johor Baharu (328,000)
Official language: Malay
Religions: Islam (53%), Buddhism (17%)
Government: Federal monarchy
Currency: Ringgit

SINGAPORE

Area: 618sq km (239sq miles)
Population: 3,104,000
Capital: Singapore (pop 2,874,000)
Official languages: Chinese, Malay, Tamil, English
Religions: Buddhism (32%), Taoism (22%), Islam (15%)
Government: Republic
Currency: Singapore dollar

BRUNEI

Area: 5,765sq km (2,226sq miles)
Population: 308,000
Capital: Bandar Seri Begawan (pop 46,000)
Official language: Malay
Religions: Islam (67%), Buddhism (13%), Christianity (10%)
Government: Monarchy
Currency: Brunei dollar

Alor Setar
Kota Baharu
George Town
Kuala Terengganu
Ipoh
Cameron Highlands
MALAYSIA
Kuantan
Kuala Lumpur
Kelang
Seremban
Straits of Malacca
Keluang
Melaka
Johor Baharu
Singapore
SINGAPORE

Exotic birds live in Malaysia, especially in the rainforests of Sabah and Sarawak. Malaysia has laws to protect wildlife and it has national parks where people can see the rich animal and plant life.

Palm oil and rubber Malaysia is the world's leading producer of palm oil which comes from the fruit of the oil palm. It also ranks among the world's major producers of natural rubber. Malaysia ranks fifth among the world's cocoa producers, although cocoa was not grown commercially there until the 1950s.

Tin mining was the industry on which Malaysia's economic development was originally based. But, in recent years, Malaysia has slipped back to third place among world tin producers after China and Indonesia.

Oil Brunei's economy depends on oil production. Malaysia also produces oil. Oil, timber and tin are its leading natural resources. Rice is the chief crop, but manufacturing is now the most valuable activity in Malaysia.

Kudat

Kota Kinabalu

Kinabalu 4094m

Sandakan

S a b a h

Bandar Seri Begawan

BRUNEI

SOUTH CHINA SEA

Kuala Belait

Tawau

Bintulu

MALAYSIA

Brunei is ruled by a Sultan who lives in a 1,700-room palace. Oil and natural gas were found in Brunei in 1929 and the nation became prosperous, making the Sultan the world's richest man. However, he lost at least half of his fortune in the 1980s and 1990s.

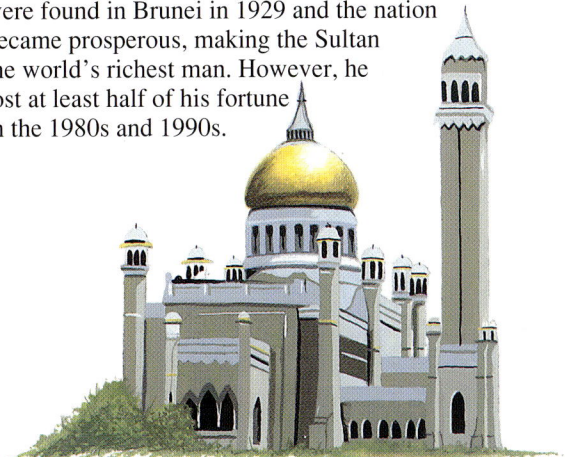

Sibu

Rajang

S a r a w a k

Kuching

Bandar Sri Aman

0   100 miles

0   100 kilometres

INDONESIA

A mainly Muslim country, Indonesia is made up of about 13,600 islands, though fewer than 6,000 are inhabited. Most of the islands are mountainous and many mountains are active volcanoes. The bigger islands also have large coastal lowlands. The country has a hot and wet climate, with large rainforests.

Indonesia became independent from the Netherlands in 1949, but Portugal continued to rule the eastern part of the island of Timor until 1975. Indonesia ruled the area from 1976 until 1999, when the local people voted to make East Timor an independent country.

Orang-utans are large apes that live in the forests of Borneo and Sumatra. They have recently been threatened by forest clearance and huge forest fires.

Banda Aceh

Medan

Mentawai Islands

Sumatra

Pakanbaru

Padang

Barisan Range

Palembang

INDIAN
OCEAN

Bangka

Tanjungkarang

Pontianak

Sintang

*Kalimantan
(Borneo)*

Samarino

Balikpapan

Belitung

Banjarmasin

I N D O

Krakatoa

Jakarta

Bogor

Java Sea

Semarang

Bandung *Java*

Surakarta

Surabaya

Yogyakarta

Malang

Bali

Lombok

Sumbawa

INDONESIA

Area: 1,904,569sq km (735,358sq miles)
Highest point: Puncak Jaya 5,030m (16,503ft)
Population: 200,390,000
Capital and largest city: Jakarta
(pop 11,500,000)
Other large cities: Surabaya (2,701,000)
Bandung (2,368,000)
Medan (1,910,000)
Palembang (1,352,000)
Official language: Bahasa Indonesia
Religions: Islam (87%), Christianity (10%)
Government: Republic
Currency: Indonesian rupiah

Tourism is an important activity in Indonesia. More than five million tourists visit the country every year. The island of Bali, with its beautiful beaches and its ancient Hindu culture, is a major tourist centre. Classical dancing is a great attraction.

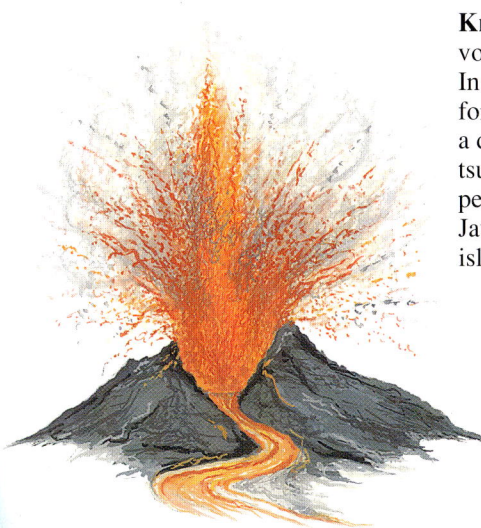

Krakatoa was one of the many volcanic islands in Indonesia. In 1883 it exploded with great force. The explosion triggered a destructive wave called a tsunami which drowned 36,000 people on nearby Sumatra and Java. About two-thirds of the island disappeared.

Spices are an important crop in Indonesia. Rice is the chief food crop and coffee, palm oil, rubber, sugar cane, tea and tobacco are exported. Agriculture employs about 44 per cent of the work force.

Jakarta, on the island of Java, is the capital of Indonesia. It is an important industrial centre and the leading economic centre of the country. Jakarta has some prosperous areas, but even more poor districts called *kampongs*. This national monument celebrates Indonesia's independence from the Netherlands.

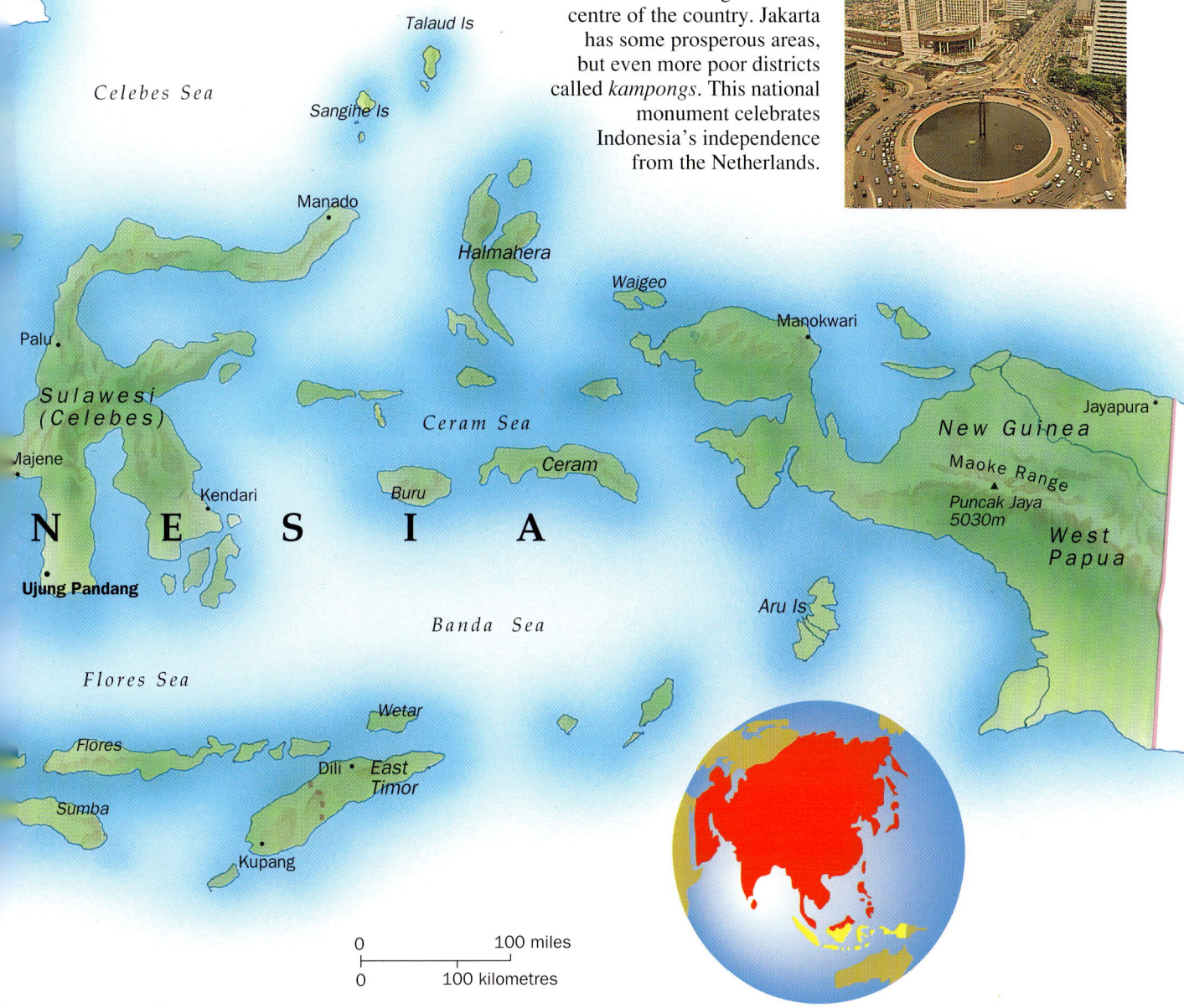

Talaud Is

Celebes Sea

Sangihe Is

Manado

Halmahera

Waigeo

Manokwari

Palu

Sulawesi (Celebes)

Ceram Sea

Ceram

Jayapura

New Guinea

Maoke Range

Puncak Jaya 5030m

Majene

Kendari

Buru

N   E   S   I   A

West Papua

Ujung Pandang

Banda Sea

Aru Is

Flores Sea

Wetar

Flores

Dili   *East Timor*

Sumba

Kupang

0 ——— 100 miles

0 ——— 100 kilometres

PHILIPPINES

The Philippines consists of about 7,100 islands, about 1,000 of which are inhabited. The country lies in the Pacific 'ring of fire', so volcanic eruptions and earthquakes are common. Much of the land is mountainous. Agriculture employs about 40 per cent of the country's workers, and bananas, cocoa, coconuts, coffee, maize, rice (the staple food), sugar cane and tobacco are leading crops. Manufacturing is increasing.

Spain ruled the Philippines from 1565 until 1898, when the United States took over. Japan invaded the Philippines during World War II, but the country became fully independent in 1946.

PHILIPPINES

Area: 300,000sq km (115,830sq miles)
Highest point: Mount Apo 2,954m (9,692ft)
Population: 73,527,000
Capital: Manila (pop 1,655,000)
Other large cities: Quezon City (1,989,000)
Caloocan (1,023,000)
Davao (961,000)
Cebu (688,000)
Official languages: Filipino, English
Religions: Christianity (Roman Catholic 83%, Protestant 5%), Islam 4.6%
Government: Republic
Currency: Philippine peso

Christianity Spain claimed the Philippines in 1565 and missionaries soon began to convert the people to Christianity. As a result, the Philippines has more Christians than any other Asian country. Here Roman Catholics gather for an open-air Communion rally.

Forests cover about one-third of the land in the Philippines. Some hardwood trees known as Philippine mahoganies provide valuable timber. The country also produces bamboo and kapok, a fibre used in upholstery.

PHILIPPINES

South China Sea

Laoag
Aparri
Luzon
Cagayan
Dagupan
Tarlac
Angeles
Olongapo
Caloocan
Quezon City
Manila
San Pab
Batangas
Mindoro
Puerto Princesa
Palawan
Sulu Sea
Balabac
Zamboang
Basilar
Jolo
Tawi-Tawi

0   100 miles
0   100 kilometres

Ferdinand Marcos (1917-89) was president of the Philippines from 1965 until 1986. Accused of corruption and election fraud, he fled the country in 1986. The Philippines faces several political problems including conflict with Muslim guerrillas, crime and unemployment.

PACIFIC OCEAN

Catanduanes

Naga

Mayon Volcano
2421m

Masbate

Samar

anay

Tacloban

Cebu   *Leyte*

Bacolod

Cebu

Dinagat

ilo

Siargao

egros   *Bohol*

Butuan

Dipolog   Cagayan de Oro

Mindanao

Pagadian

Datu Piang   **Davao**

Apo
2954m

General Santos

Jeepneys are a popular means of transport in the Philippines. These highly decorated shared taxis provide cheap transport for their passengers, who are crammed in. Buses are also important.

Manila, the capital of the Philippines, is also the country's chief commercial and cultural centre, as well as being the main port. It is a beautiful city on the shores of Manila Bay on Luzon island, but it has many slums where people live in desperate poverty.

Philippine eagles are also called monkey-eating eagles. They are found only in the Philippines. These eagles eat not just monkeys but also other mammals, birds and reptiles.They are becoming scarce because the rainforest trees in which they nest are being cut down.

Sugar cane grows well in the fertile, volcanic soils of the Philippines. Sugar cane is a plant that belongs to the grass family. Its stalks contain a sweet juice from which sugar and syrup are made.

PEOPLE AND BELIEFS

More than 60 per cent of the world's people live in Asia. Vast areas are too dry, too cold or too mountainous for people to live in them. By contrast, some parts of eastern, southeastern and southern Asia are among the most densely populated places in the world. Many people live in huge cities. Asia's largest cities include Tokyo (Japan), Jakarta (Indonesia), Seoul (South Korea), Mumbai (formerly Bombay, in India), Shanghai (China) and Delhi (India).

The Dome of the Rock mosque rises above the Wailing Wall in Jerusalem. Islam, Hinduism and Buddhism are the main faiths in Asia. There are fewer than five million Jews.

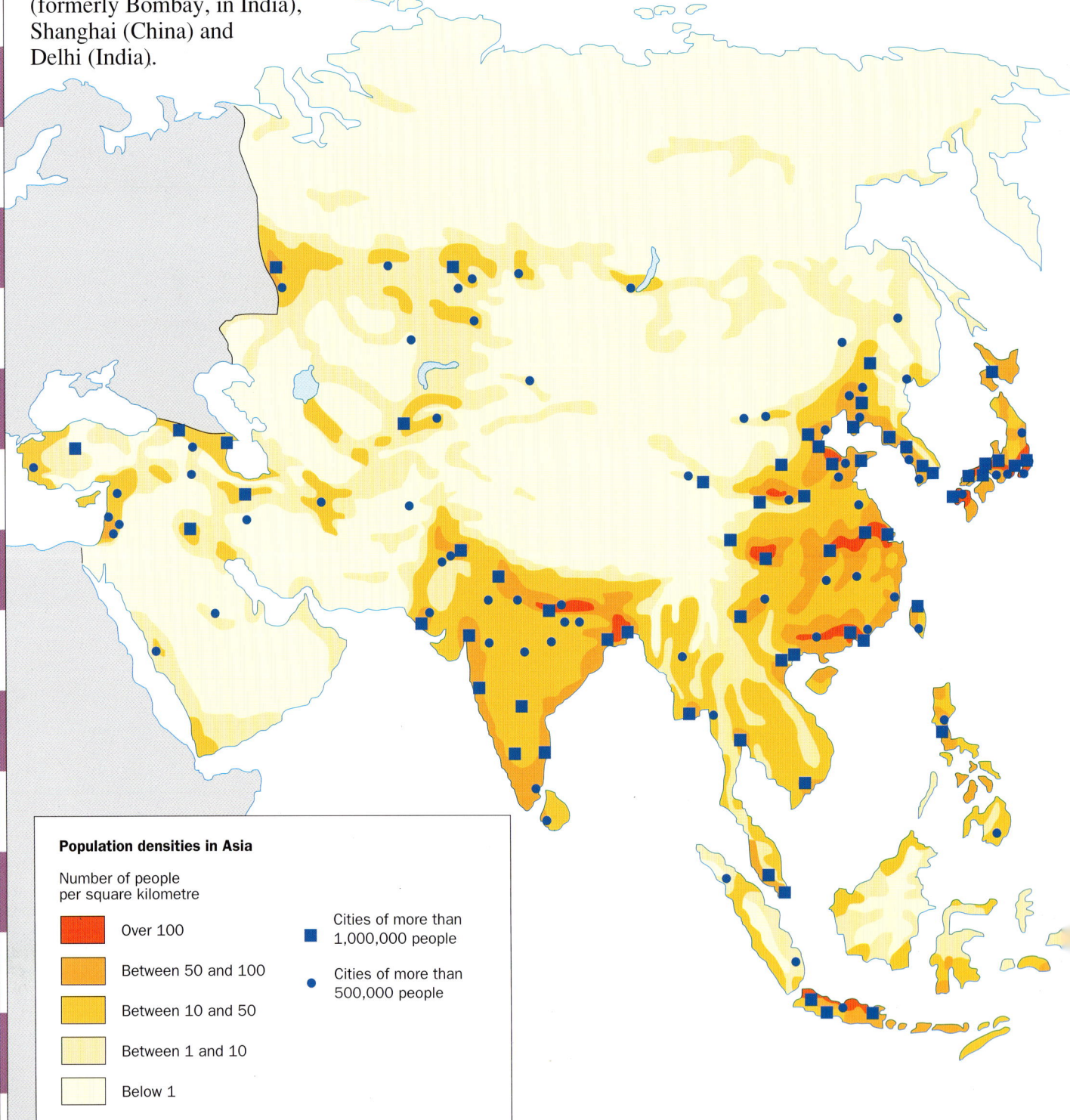

Population densities in Asia

Number of people per square kilometre

- Over 100
- Between 50 and 100
- Between 10 and 50
- Between 1 and 10
- Below 1

- Cities of more than 1,000,000 people
- Cities of more than 500,000 people

Population and area

Although only 75 per cent of Russia lies in Asia, it is Asia's largest country. The next largest countries in Asia are China, India, Kazakhstan (a small proportion of which is in Europe), Saudi Arabia and the island country of Indonesia.

China and India have more people than any other countries in the world. Indonesia ranks fourth, after the United States. Russia ranks sixth in population, but about 80 per cent of Russia's population lives in European Russia. Pakistan, Japan and Bangladesh also have huge populations.

Percentage of population of Asia by country

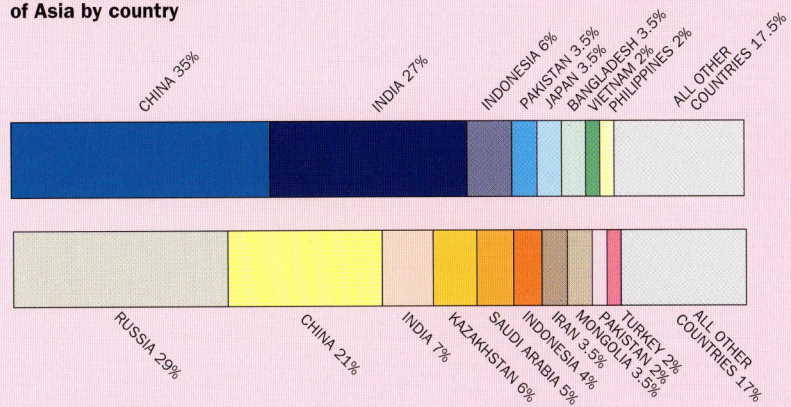

CHINA 35% · INDIA 27% · INDONESIA 6% · PAKISTAN 3.5% · JAPAN 3.5% · BANGLADESH 3.5% · VIETNAM 2% · PHILIPPINES 2% · ALL OTHER COUNTRIES 17.5%

RUSSIA 29% · CHINA 21% · INDIA 7% · KAZAKHSTAN 6% · SAUDI ARABIA 5% · INDONESIA 4% · IRAN 3.5% · MONGOLIA 3.5% · PAKISTAN 2% · TURKEY 2% · ALL OTHER COUNTRIES 17%

Areas of countries within Asia

Main religions

All the world's major religions were founded in Asia. Judaism, Christianity and Islam all began in southwestern Asia. Today, most people in southwestern Asia are Muslims, but Judaism is the chief religion in Israel and Christianity the chief religion in Cyprus. Hinduism began in India and, today, more than four-fifths of the people of India are Hindus. But Muslims make up about 12 per cent of the people of India, while Islam is also the chief religion in Bangladesh, the Maldives and Pakistan. Buddhism, which began in India about 2,500 years ago, has spread into much of eastern Asia. Islam is the chief religion of Brunei, Indonesia and Malaysia, while Christianity is the main religion in the Philippines. Some local religions survive in remote areas in Indonesia. Confucianism is important in eastern Asia, while Shinto is followed in Japan.

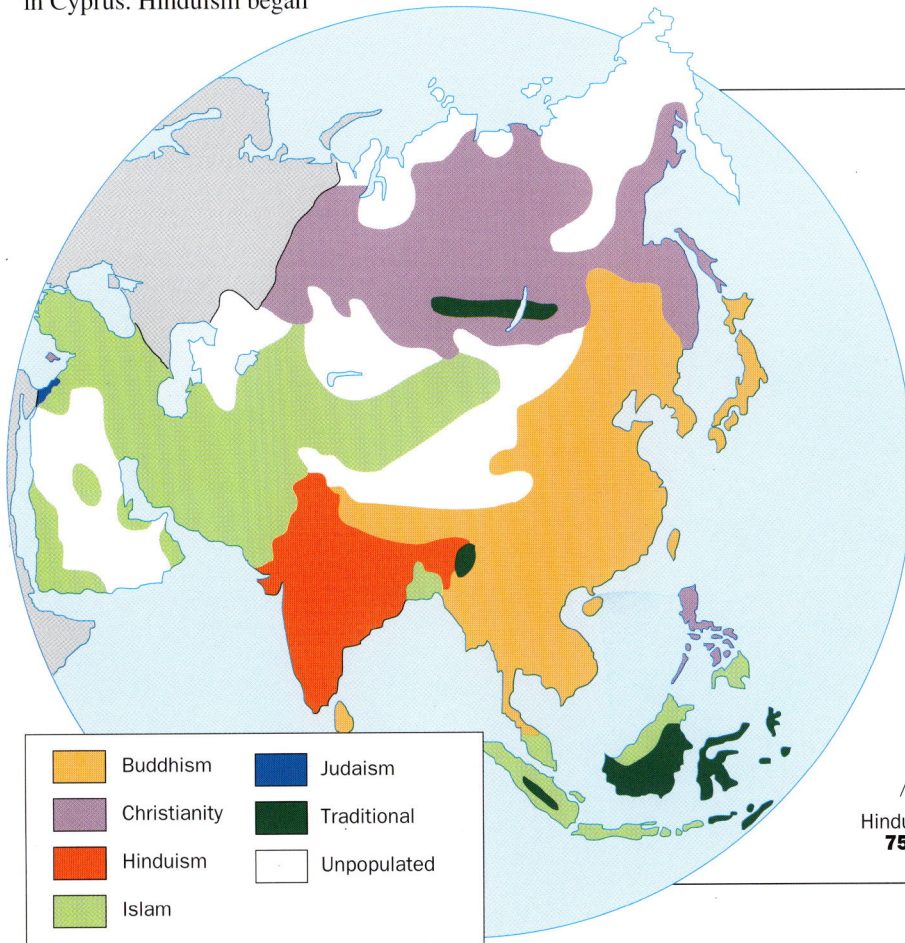

Buddhism	Judaism
Christianity	Traditional
Hinduism	Unpopulated
Islam	

Main religious groups in Asia
(number of followers in millions in 1997)

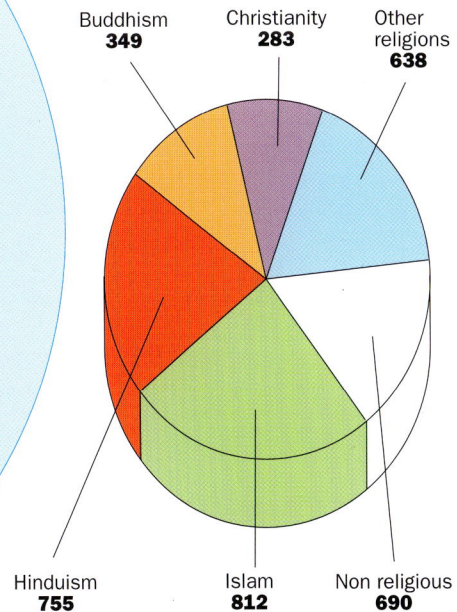

Buddhism **349** · Christianity **283** · Other religions **638** · Hinduism **755** · Islam **812** · Non religious **690**

CLIMATE AND VEGETATION

Asia's climates range from polar and tundra in the north, to hot tropical in the south. South of the polar region, much of Siberia, in northern Asia, has a cold climate, with vast coniferous forests of fir, pine and spruce. In eastern Asia, these forests merge into mixed forest, with tropical forests in the southeast and parts of India. Central Asia has grassy steppe and cold deserts, while hot deserts cover much of southwestern Asia.

Land use
(excluding Russia)

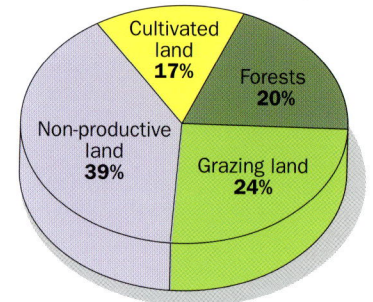

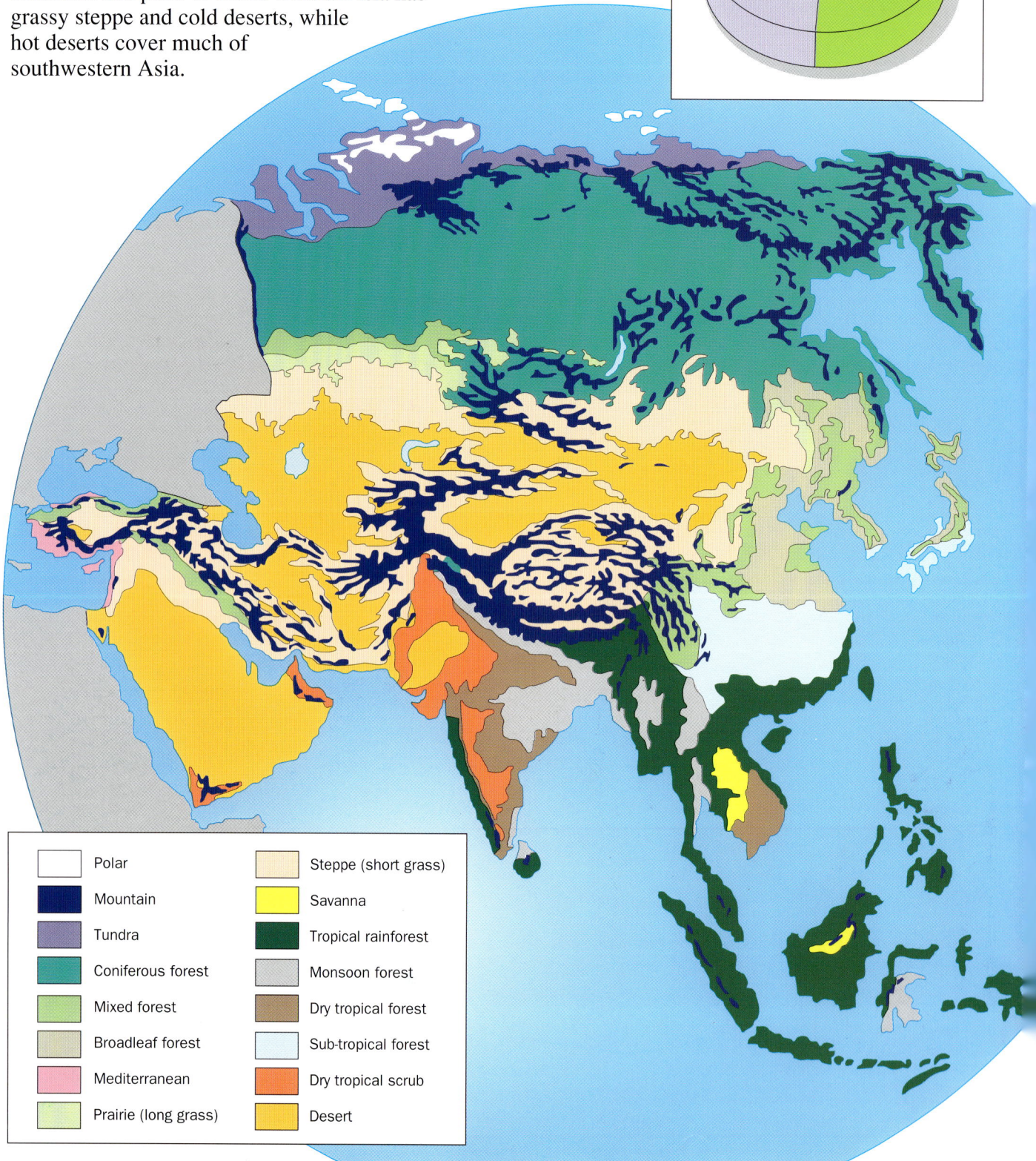

- Cultivated land **17%**
- Forests **20%**
- Grazing land **24%**
- Non-productive land **39%**

Legend:

- Polar
- Mountain
- Tundra
- Coniferous forest
- Mixed forest
- Broadleaf forest
- Mediterranean
- Prairie (long grass)
- Steppe (short grass)
- Savanna
- Tropical rainforest
- Monsoon forest
- Dry tropical forest
- Sub-tropical forest
- Dry tropical scrub
- Desert

Winter temperatures

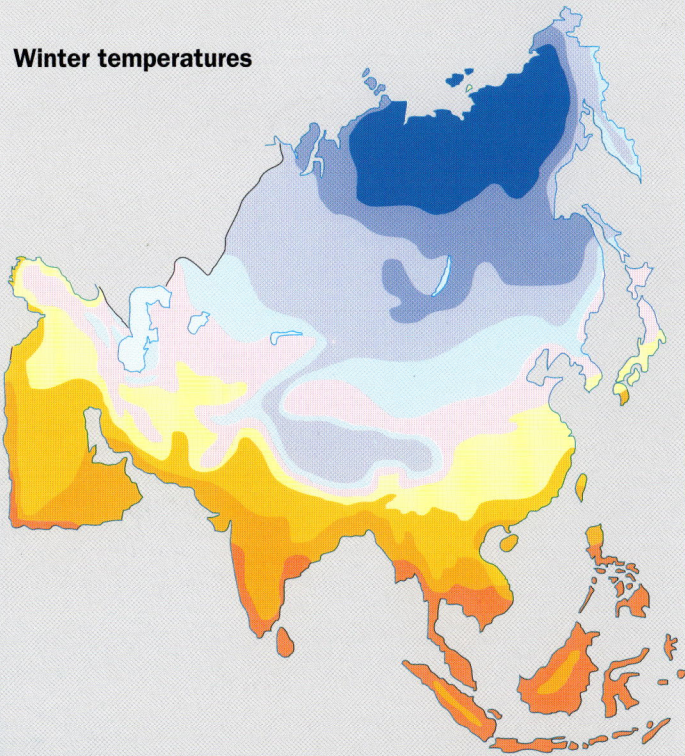

Temperature
key scale in °C

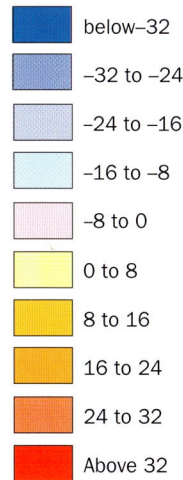

	below -32
	-32 to -24
	-24 to -16
	-16 to -8
	-8 to 0
	0 to 8
	8 to 16
	16 to 24
	24 to 32
	Above 32

Range of climates

Temperature and precipitation (rain, snow and all other forms of moisture that come from the air) are the two main factors that determine climate. Asia's climate varies from the Arctic north to the equatorial regions in the southeast. The climate is influenced by the distance a place is from the sea. Extreme climates, with hot summers and bitterly cold winters and little precipitation, occur in central Asia.

In southern Asia, winds blow outwards from the land to the sea in winter. In summer, the land heats up and moist air is drawn inland from the sea. This causes a reversal of wind directions. These seasonal winds are called monsoons.

Rainfall

Monsoons bring heavy rain to India and other areas in summer. Indonesia has rain throughout the year, while southwestern Asia has a hot desert climate. Life is possible only at oases – places where water is available.

Floods and droughts

Heavy monsoon rains sometimes make rivers overflow, causing floods. When the monsoon winds are late or fail to bring enough rain, droughts may occur. Crops fail and people may suffer starvation.

Annual rainfall
in mm

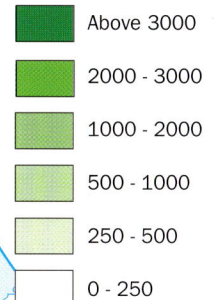

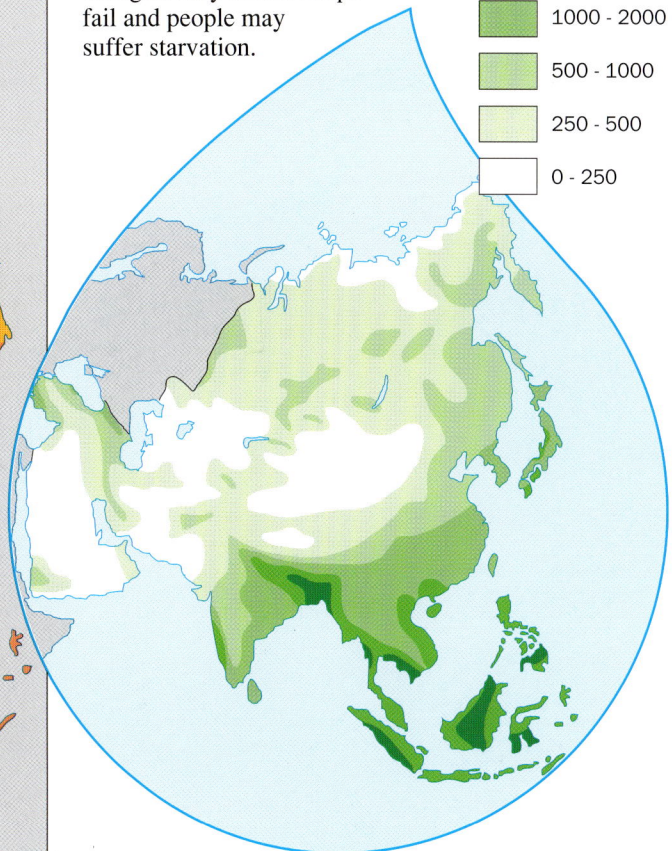

	Above 3000
	2000 - 3000
	1000 - 2000
	500 - 1000
	250 - 500
	0 - 250

Summer temperatures

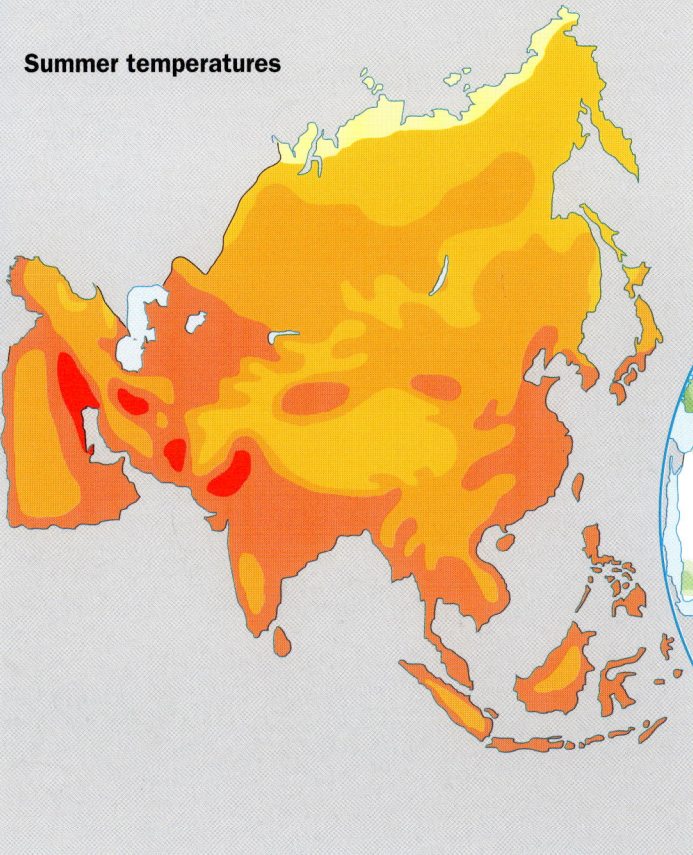

ECOLOGY AND ENVIRONMENT

Currently Asia's population is increasing every year by more than 50 million. Many parts of Asia are overcrowded and, as the population increases, overcrowding grows worse. The yearly increase in population creates pressure on the land, with rainforests being cleared to provide timber and fuel, and land for farming and human settlement. In some areas, the cutting down of trees has led to environmental disasters and a great reduction in the numbers of wild animals and plants. Unknown numbers of plant species, some that might have been of medicinal value, become extinct all the time.

Rice is harvested on land that was once rainforest. The people need the food, but the environmental cost is unknown.

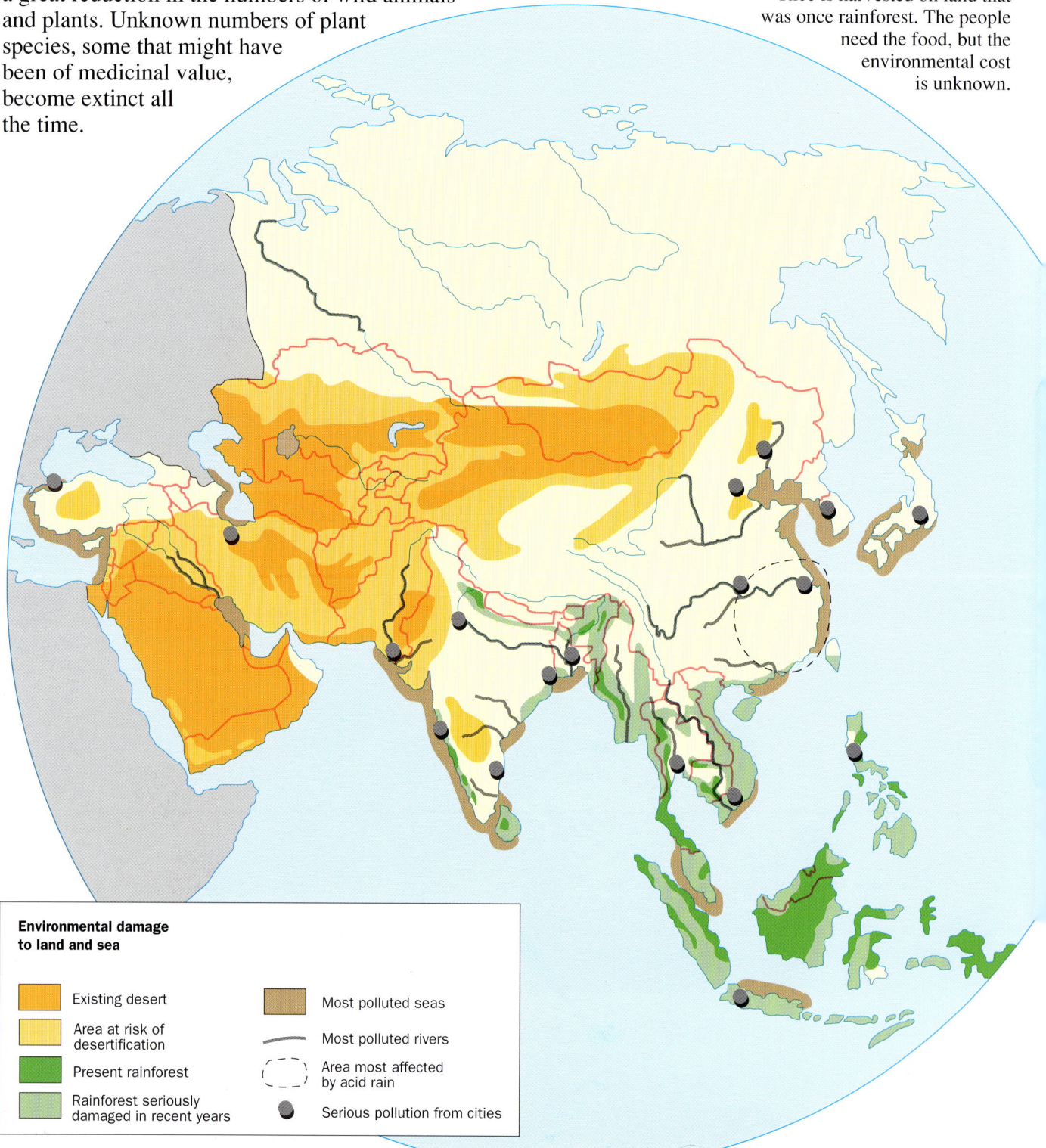

Environmental damage to land and sea

- Existing desert
- Area at risk of desertification
- Present rainforest
- Rainforest seriously damaged in recent years
- Most polluted seas
- Most polluted rivers
- Area most affected by acid rain
- Serious pollution from cities

Damaging the environment

When forests in upland areas are cut down, the effects are felt in the lowlands. Without trees to soak up the water and anchor the soil, the rain flows over the surface, washing away fertile soils. The soil is swept into the swollen rivers, where it piles up on the river beds. This makes the rivers overflow their banks, causing floods. Serious floods occurred in Bangladesh in 2000.

In the late 1990s, forest fires in Indonesia, many deliberately started to clear the land, caused clouds of smoke that choked people in countries to the north, such as Malaysia and Singapore.

In Asia's overcrowded cities, factories and cars fill the air with gases, causing severe air pollution. Factories also tip harmful chemicals into rivers, making the water poisonous. Human populations use the river water for washing and also for disposing of waste. But the rivers are unable to cope with the amount of pollution and clean water is becoming increasingly scarce.

Natural hazards

Earthquakes occur in a band stretching from Turkey to the Himalayas. Earthquakes and volcanic eruptions are also common in southeastern and eastern Asia, which forms part of the Pacific 'ring of fire' where movements between the earth's crustal plates occur. The world's worst natural disaster in historic times was an earthquake in Shanxi province, in northern China, in 1556. About 830,000 people died.

Tropical storms, which drive seawater inland, causing floods, are another hazard facing the poor in southern and southeastern Asia. In 1970, a storm in Bangladesh killed about a million people.

Endangered species

The natural habitats of many animals have been greatly reduced as the human population has increased. Many kinds of animals are now endangered. The most famous example is the giant panda, the symbol of the World Wide Fund for Nature. It lives in what remains of the cold forests in China's Sichuan province. Most of the trees and bamboos have been cut down by local people to build homes and for firewood.

Many animals, such as tigers and monkeys, are hunted by poachers for their skins and for body parts that are used in folk medicines. Some, including orang-utans, are caught as babies and sold as pets. Orang-utans have also been threatened by forest clearance and uncontrolled fires. Some species, including the large birdwing butterflies and many rainforest trees, are now protected.

Javan rhinoceros

Some endangered species of Asia

Birds
Gurney's pitta
Japanese crane
Philippine monkey-eating eagle
Rothschild's mynah

Mammals and reptiles
Asian elephant
Giant panda
Javan and Sumatran rhinos
Komodo dragon
Orang-utan
River terrapin
Tiger

Plants and trees
Blue vanda orchid
Dove tree
Paphiopedilum orchid
Rafflesia arnoldii

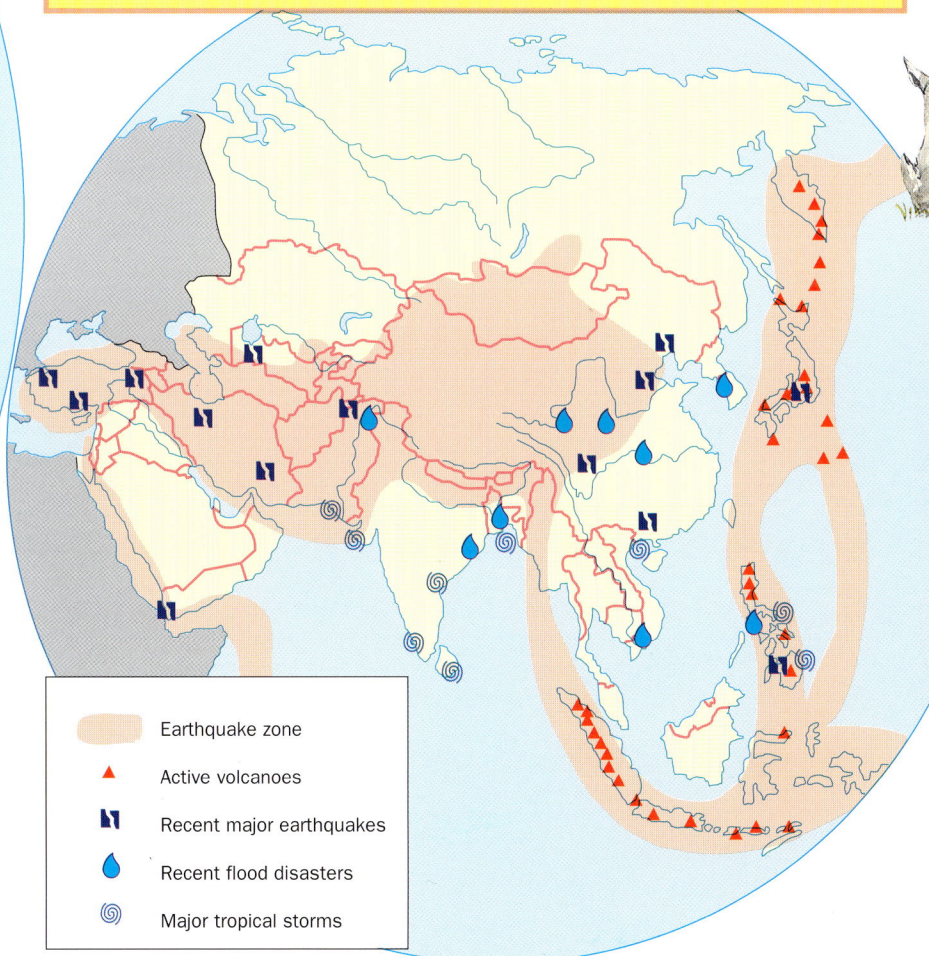

Earthquake zone
Active volcanoes
Recent major earthquakes
Recent flood disasters
Major tropical storms

ECONOMY

More than half the people of Asia make their living by farming.
Many farmers are poor and grow little more than they need to
feed their families. The use of machinery, fertilizers and new,
higher-producing seeds of such crops as rice and wheat,
have raised production in recent years. Japan is a major
industrial power and manufacturing is increasing,
especially in eastern Asia, from
Indonesia to Korea.

All over Asia old-fashioned factories are
being modernized to cope with increasing
trade with the rest of the world.

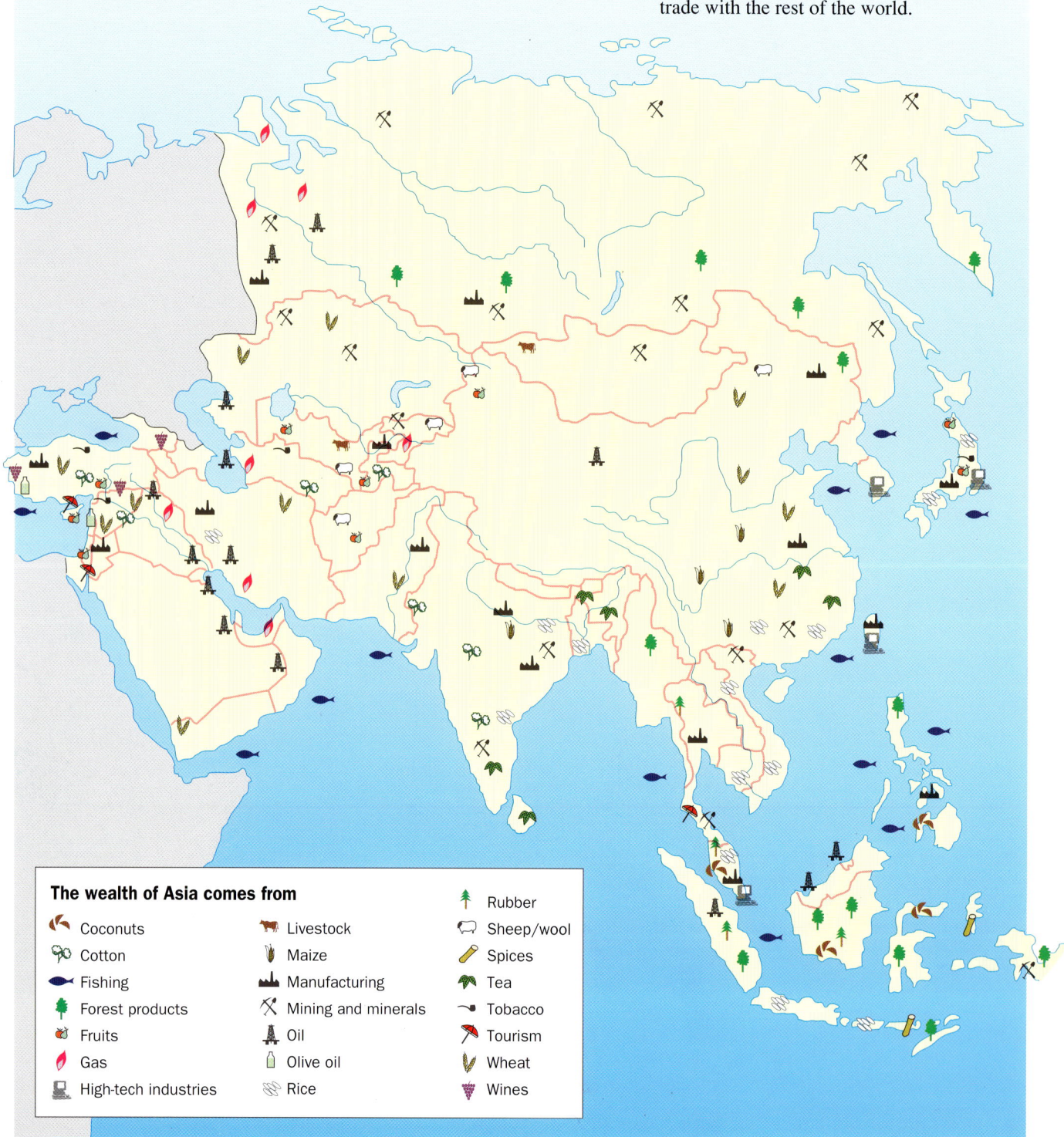

The wealth of Asia comes from

Coconuts	Livestock	Rubber
Cotton	Maize	Sheep/wool
Fishing	Manufacturing	Spices
Forest products	Mining and minerals	Tea
Fruits	Oil	Tobacco
Gas	Olive oil	Tourism
High-tech industries	Rice	Wheat
		Wines

Gross national product

In order to compare the economies of countries, experts work out the gross national product (GNP) of the countries in US dollars. The GNP is the total value of the goods and services produced by a country in a year. The chart shows that Japan has the highest GNP. Its GNP ranks second only in the world to that of the United States. It is more than four times larger than the GNP of China and more than 13 times larger than the GNP of India.

GNP for the countries of Asia (in billions of dollars)

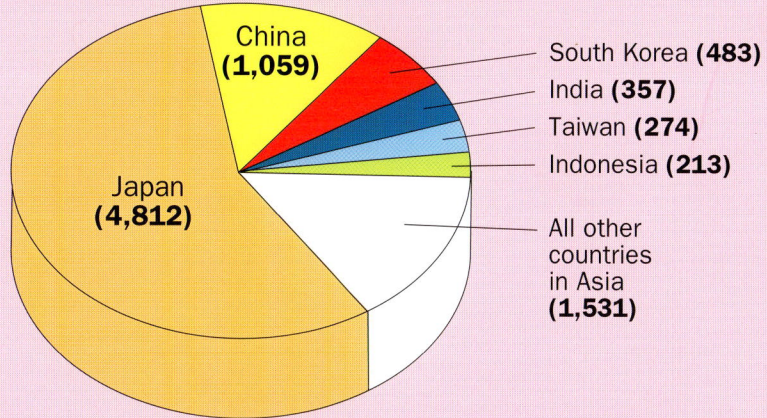

China (1,059)
Japan (4,812)
South Korea (483)
India (357)
Taiwan (274)
Indonesia (213)
All other countries in Asia (1,531)

Sources of energy

Several of Asia's leading industrial countries, including Japan, lack oil, natural gas and coal. They have to import these fuels to produce the energy they need. Several Asian countries are, however, major fuel producers. Southwestern Asia is a leading source of oil. Saudi Arabia leads the world in oil production and it contains the largest known reserves. Iran and the United Arab Emirates also ranked among the world's top ten producers in 1996, as did China and Russia. Russia, Indonesia, Uzbekistan and Saudi Arabia are also major producers of natural gas. China leads the world in coal production, while India, Russia and Kazakhstan are other leading coal producers.

Per capita GNPs

Per capita means per head or per person. Per capita GNPs are worked out by dividing the GNP by the population. Japan has the highest per capita GNP in Asia, but tiny Singapore, with its many industries, also has a high per capita GNP. Countries with low per capita GNPs are Afghanistan, Cambodia, Nepal and Yemen.

Sources of energy found in Asia

- Oil
- Gas
- Hydroelectricity
- Coal
- Uranium

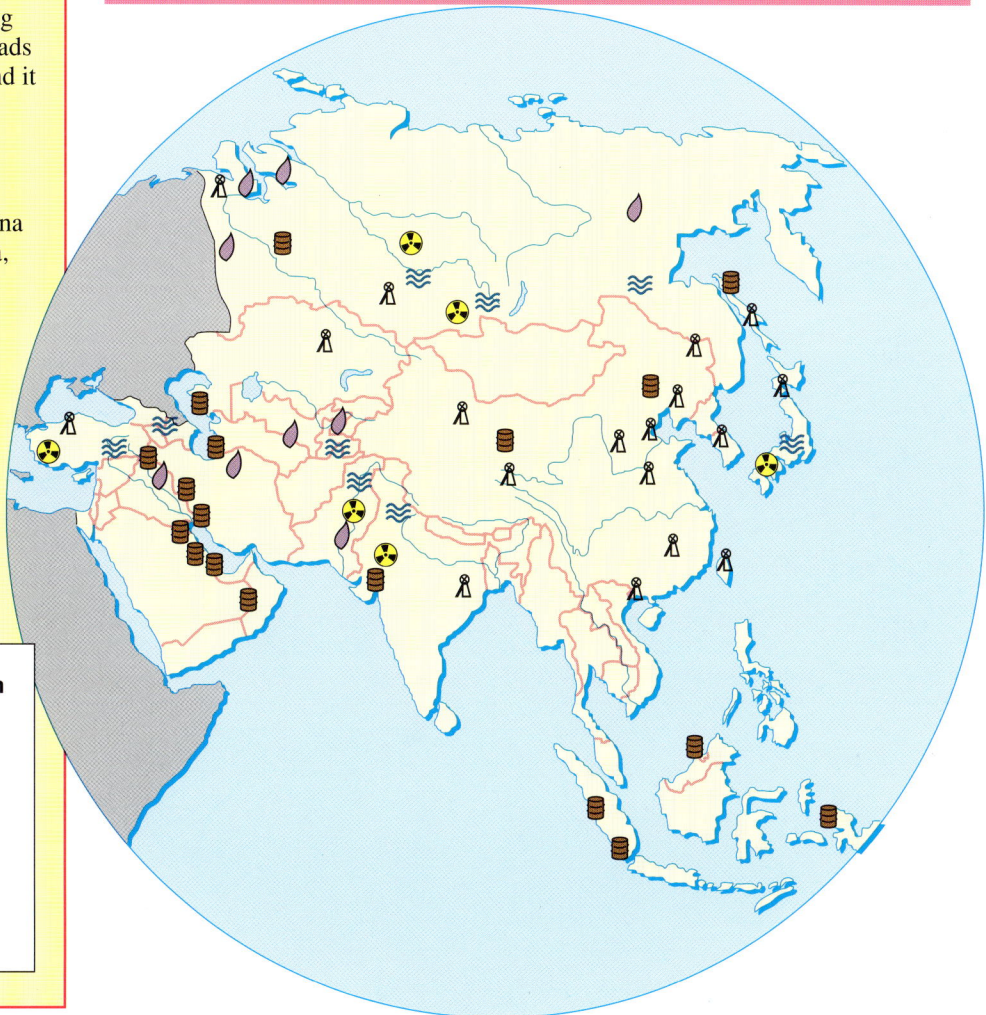

POLITICS AND HISTORY

The world map is always changing. From the 1940s, country after country in Asia became independent. In 1947 British India was divided into India and Pakistan. These two countries still dispute their boundaries. In 1991 the nations of Kazakhstan, Kyrgyzstan, Tajikistan, Turkmenistan and Uzbekistan were created when the Soviet Union split up. In 1997, British Hong Kong became part of China and, in 1999, the people of East Timor voted to break away from Indonesia.

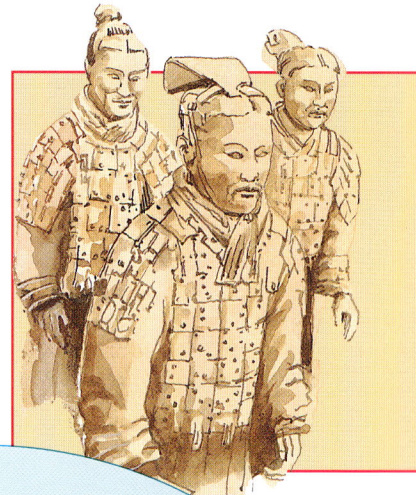

Great events

The oldest known civilizations were founded in Mesopotamia in what is now Iraq. Other great civilizations grew up in the Indus River valley and in north and central China. Asia is also the home of the world's major religions.

Contact with Europe increased rapidly from the early 16th century when the Portuguese found new sea routes from Europe to Asia. Following the Portuguese came Spanish, Dutch and British traders and missionaries, while at the same time Russia spread its influence across Siberia. By the 19th century, European powers had colonized much of Asia. In the late 19th and early 20th centuries, Japan emerged as a military power, but it was defeated in 1945, when the first atomic bombs were dropped on the country.

In the late 1940s, several Asian countries became independent and, in 1949, a Communist government took over in China. The spread of Communism led to wars in such places as Korea (1950-3) and Vietnam (1954-75). Japan, with help from the United States, recovered to become a major world economic power. From the 1970s, several countries, including Hong Kong (part of China since 1997), South Korea, Singapore, Taiwan and Thailand, have built up their economies. Many Asians remain poor. The fight against poverty is Asia's main challenge in the 21st century.

Great Asian empires

- 🟩 Assyrian 700 BC
- 🟥 Ch'in 200 BC
- 🟨 Mongol 1300
- 🟦 Mughal 1700

Important dates

8350 Jericho founded – the world's first walled city

6000 First known pottery and textiles at Çatal Hüyük (Turkey)

3500 Mesopotamian empires founded in Iraq

3100 First writing on clay tablets from Mesopotamia

2750 Growth of Indus Valley civilizations

2500 Horses domesticated in central Asia

1700s Huange He and Yangtze civilizations in China

1600 Rise of Shang dynasty in China

720 Height of Assyrian Empire

660 Jimmu, first emperor of Japan

486 Death of Siddhartha Gautama, founder of Buddhism

300s Empire of Alexander the Great

214 Great Wall of China built

200s Ch'in Empire in China

AD 30 Jesus of Nazareth, founder of Christianity, crucified in Jerusalem

100s Han Empire of China

300s Gupta Empire of China

407 Start of first Mongol Empire

625 Islam founded by the Prophet Mohammed

700s Tang Empire of China

730 First printing in China

939 Civil wars in Japan

1096 First crusades to the Holy Land

1206 Genghis Khan conquered largest empire in history

1275 Marco Polo established merchant route by land from Europe to China

1368 Ming dynasty founded in China

1516 Height of Ottoman (Turkish) Empire

8000 BC	AD 1	1500

Asia has seen many great empires. Hundreds of statues of warriors made from terracotta (clay) have been unearthed near the Chinese city of Xi'an. This terracotta army was made to guard the tomb of a Chinese emperor who died more than 2,200 years ago.

Centre of
Mongol Empire
covering most of
Asia by 1300

Korean War
1950-3

**Great Wall
of China**
begun in 5th
century BC

**Chinese
Revolution**
1911-49

Japan
First nuclear
weapons used
1945

Mesopotamia
Empires founded
3500 BC

Israel
founded
1948

Iraq
invaded Kuwait
1990

Afghanistan
invaded by
Russia 1979

**Mahatma
Gandhi**
assassinated
1948

Bangladesh
Many thousands
died in floods
2000

Hong Kong
reunited with
China 1997

Vietnam War
1954-75

Krakatoa
massive volcanic
eruption 1883

East Timor
voted for
independence
1999

1526 Foundation of Mughal Empire in India
1539 Death of Kabir Narrak, founder of Sikh religion
1600s Dutch colonized Indonesia
1630 Japan isolated itself from the rest of the world
1700s Manchu Empire in China
1747 Kingdom of Afghanistan founded
1757 British colonized India
1800s French colonized Indochina
1819 Foundation of Singapore
1854 Trade treaty between Japan and USA
1911-49 Chinese Revolution
1917 Russian Revolution
1924 Mongolia became Communist
1934 Mao Zedong led Long March to Shanxi
1941 Japanese attacked Pearl Harbor
1945 First nuclear weapons used in Japan
1946-9 Communists won Civil War in China
1947 India and Pakistan became independent
1948 Jewish State of Israel founded;
Mahatma Gandhi assassinated in India
1949 Indonesia became independent
1950-3 Korean War
1954-75 Vietnam War
1957 Malaysia became independent
1971 East Pakistan became independent as Bangladesh
1975 Civil war in Lebanon
1979 Russia invaded Afghanistan; Islamic revolution in Iran
1984 Indira Gandhi, Indian Prime Minister, assassinated
1990 Gulf War after Iraqi invasion of Kuwait
1995 Israeli Prime Minister, Yitzhak Rabin assassinated
1997 Hong Kong returned to Chinese rule
1999 East Timorese voted for independence

2000

INDEX

Numbers in **bold** are map references
Numbers in *italics* are picture references

Picture credits
Photographs: David Scott 26, 42
The Hutchison Library 8, 13, 15, 17, 21, 22, 23, 34,
   35, 36